U0148010

Set Love Free
逐自由之愛

Female Sexuality as Subversive Agency in Lord Byron's *Don Juan*

拜倫《唐璜》中女性情慾反叛之能動性

Cheng-Fen Chen

陳正芬

Set Love Free: Female Sexuality as Subversive Agency in Lord Byron's *Don Juan* / Cheng-Fen Chen（陳正芬）著. -- 初版. -- 高雄市：麗文文化, 2022.03
面； 公分
ISBN 978-986-490-178-4

Set Love Free: Female Sexuality as Subversive Agency in Lord Byron's *Don Juan*

初版一刷・2022年3月3日

作　　者　Cheng-Fen Chen（陳正芬）
封面設計　余旻禎
發 行 人　楊曉祺
總 編 輯　蔡國彬
出 版 者　麗文文化事業股份有限公司
地　　址　80252高雄市苓雅區五福一路57號2樓之2
電　　話　07-2265267
傳　　真　07-2264697
網　　址　www.liwen.com.tw
電子信箱　liwen@liwen.com.tw
劃撥帳號　41423894
購書專線　07-2265267轉236
臺北分公司　100003台北市中正區重慶南路一段57號10樓之12
電　　話　02-29222396
傳　　真　02-29220464
法律顧問　林廷隆律師
電　　話　02-29658212
行政院新聞局出版事業登記證局版台業字第5692號
ISBN：9789864901784

麗文文化事業

定價：新臺幣380元

Set Love Free

Female Sexuality as Subversive Agency in Lord Byron's *Don Juan*

Author: Cheng-Fen Chen

Publisher: Liwen Publishers Co., Ltd

Address: 2F.-2, No.57, Wufu 1st Rd., Lingya Dist., Kaohsiung City, 802019, Taiwan(R.O.C)

Tel: 886-7-2236780/2265267/2236383

Fax: 886-7-2264697

e-mail: liwen@liwen.com.tw

Website: http://www.liwen.com.tw

Chief Editor: Guo-Bin Tsai

Art Editor: Ming-Chen Yu

Publish Date: March 3, 2022 (1st edition)

List Price: NTD 380

ISBN: 9789864901784

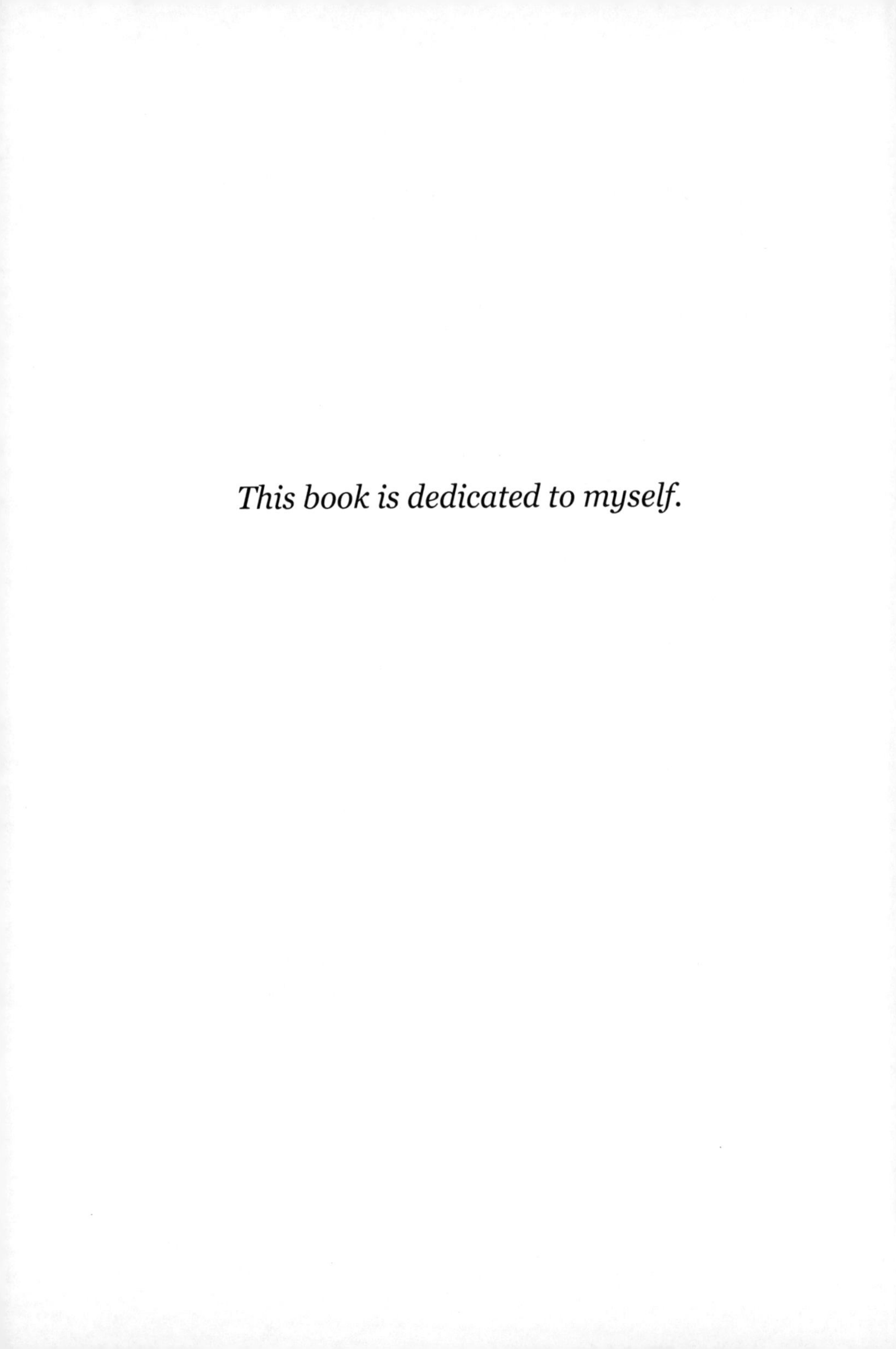

This book is dedicated to myself.

Love may make you a true legend.

—— *Cheng-Fen Chen*

Aesthetics

March, not so cold.
Sun helps the sky slowly. Art and skyline
are engrossed together.

There is no disturbed feelings of national subjugation.
Use sea tides continually
to make up the bare face.

"For the deep feeling, fishes under the sea know that the conflict must exist."

Every day, breathing young-like green.
Inquiry becomes feedback.
My imagination never loses its magic.
The writing answers coming behind, like art,
eventually elaborate their romantic thinking layers by layers.

The young girl adult looked into the mirror,
finding the night-frightened gazing during the day.
The tranquility keeps me,
telling me:

Flying to the sky this time,
you will not fall—
a kind of "not at all."

The coast has the most shining broken stones melted.

—— *Cheng-Fen Chen*

Wandering in Fall

The Green shade on both sides is like a forest lining fresh.
Qin Mei Calligraphy Greenway looked as if it was telling Nordic fairy tales.
Buildings also become one of the beautiful elements.
The comfort and energy in early Fall
belong to Romanticism.
Fluorescent transparent bubbles display the beauty of nature.
Blessings fall everywhere.
Going through youth and toward more mature age,
we push the sun by our light footsteps and
believe that ideals are also on the path,
revealing
novelty and intellectuality.

Walking toward the end of the road,
we talk until the stars
cannot be seen even with the telescopes.
And we grab for the stars again.
The stars, in our hands, indicate the most wonderful
self-exiles.

Before the end of Fall,

I will pick up the core ideals

with you.

Wandering around the fallen leaves,

we not merely

cultivate loneliness with our deep hearts.

Even before the sun goes down from a high place,

we feel the tranquility

of the cascading leaves and flowers.

—— *Cheng-Fen Chen*

Recommendation

The author, through her analysis of the rhetorical and formal characteristics of Byron's *Don Juan*, is able to reveal the importance of Byron's view of female sexuality and female emancipation. This is an aspect of the work that is often overlooked, and I believe that she is able to convincingly demonstrate its importance and even, in a sense, its centrality for the work's overall vision. She supports her arguments with references to a range of contemporary thinkers, but continually anchors her conclusions in careful examinations of the various female figures in the poem and in Byron's view of them, both explicit and more subtly implied. Her appreciation of the poem's well-known digressive form also adds credence to her argument. Ultimately she is able to reveal a previously unsuspected dimension of this work, namely, Byron's view of the importance of female sexuality and female emancipation. In doing so, she throws a new and interesting light on an otherwise familiar work which, I believe, will make it even more interesting for many contemporary readers.

—— Steven Frattali, Former Assistent Professor, DFLL, NTHU, American Writer

Recommendation

The author leads readers to reread and reinterpret Byron's *Don Juan* from highly creative viewpoints. Through the analysis of Byron's unruly freedom claims, she also thinks deeply about love, female autonomy, and the consciousness of resisting patriarchy. In the complex narrative structure of *Don Juan*, the author has mastered the factors of travel and time, together with post-structuralism arguments to demonstrate the relationship between lovers and the stranger Don Juan. Their love has a complex mental framework, which reveals the personalities of Romantic Poets: they are eager to grasp the passion for love. This is indeed a poetic dissertation full of brand-new arguments.

—— Wen-Wei Shiu, Poet, Professor, Department of Chinese, NTNU

推薦語

作者以相當具有創造力的觀點，帶領讀者重新閱讀與詮釋拜倫的《唐璜》，透過分析詩人不羈的自由主張，也省思愛情、女性的自主與抵抗父權的意識。在《唐璜》複雜的敘事結構中，作者掌握了旅行與時間的因素，以後結構主義的論點，論證戀人與異鄉人唐璜的關係，有著複雜的心理框架，呈現出浪漫主義詩人個性的張揚，歌頌與把握愛情的熱切，是一本充滿嶄新論點的詩學論述。

——須文蔚・詩人・國立臺灣師範大學國文學系教授

Praise for Set Love Free

A must-collect book for any Byron admires. *Set Love Free* and Emily's poetic works give you all the affectionate insight you can feel in love. This book is really a unique artwork.

—— Chiou-Ling Shi

The opinions and research results provided in this book are precious. Beautiful, passionate, and sentimental to know.

—— Leslie Chang

Emily Chen has achieved an enlightening discourse on Byron's *Don Juan*. Also, her works are so sincere that you can feel the distinctive romantic spirits. Emily is a diligent writer, and she could write various articles. Absolutely emotional and rational!

—— Kevin Chuang

If you are attracted to the Byronic Hero, you must not miss this book. I got strength from the outstanding discourse and from the romantic poems: both artistic and enlightening.

—— Redmuhly33

Preface

"Man's love is of man's life a thing apart, 'Tis woman's whole existence" is a famous quote from Byron's *Don Juan*. It is clear that Byron's love affairs occupied most of his life; moreover, such a personal history of love inspired him to create a variety of works in which women played a crucial role. Byron's *Don Juan* not only shows colorful romances but also reveals women's desires and sexualities in a positive way. This book is a representation of how women become more individualized and sophisticated through their active pursuit of love in *Don Juan*. Meanwhile, the inherent tensions of the satiric tones are the narrator's rhetorical means of compelling readers to see reality from different perspectives. Within a larger framework of satire, the issue of female sexuality and the concept of love are easily assumed a darker color. In fact, Byron's usage of a comic tone does not satirize women; instead, he describes how wonderful love is in the world through images of women in love and the emotions that are the original desires of human beings. Love is spiritual enrichment of one's daily life and a kind of symbol of energy and happiness. In addition, the author presents women's gradual getting rid of social constraints and developing their confidence. Their experiences of love offer unlimited possibilities for shaping their own identities and result in a kind of spiritual transcendence from which the new thinking and meanings of life are generated.

What Byron would like to show in *Don Juan* is the exploration of human feelings, especially human passions and the nature of love. In the context of Byron's arguments against despotism, he thinks that one's sexuality and desire about love must be free. Traditionally, women's connection with love is conservative and supposed to be passive. Women become a target for men to choose as part of their lives. However, Byron transforms such a fixed stereotype and depicts female's active performance in the quest for love. Using satire, Byron presents more accurate concepts of love, human beings, and true freedom. Implicit in the poem is that the nature of love is a kind of desire which exists in everyone's heart. Based on Byron's devotion to liberty, female sexuality is worth admiring and should not be regulated by external limits from society, politics, and morality. Under such a revolutionary intention, the spirit of "carpe diem" is also revised and given a new meaning: it shows not only the hedonic aspect of life but also the extreme effort to change one's condition. There is no hierarchy in the world of love; women also can dominate men for the sake of true love and happiness they want. Time and physical beauty are fleeting, so just make the most present pleasure and fulfillment count. Thus, Byron's revolutionary and rebellious spirits are obvious here: he adopts ironic tone to criticize orthodox ideas. He portrays an ideal equality between men and women.

This book is divided into four chapters. And I put my own romantic poems in each chapter foreword, showing a proper fusion of lovely thinking. Byron tries to tell readers that seizing the time to love is very important. Especially as a woman, she should bravely chase her happiness regardless of gender, class, race, and other oppressive elements because love is a kind of strong feeling which happens in a sudden moment without reasons or explanations. At last, Byron's attitude toward love echoes the typical thinking of Romanticism—"Sentimental emotion is over everything"—the strength and extreme value of love can save both men and women. Therefore, true freedom and fulfillment for women do contribute to equality between men and women.

Contents

Second A Color of Your Eyes

The silent moment
attracted huge vibration of my mind.
You, oncoming with the vibes,
eventualy see me through.
What exactly does the figurative
want to create?
Do not let the eye contact between us become the only demand.

—— *Cheng-Fen Chen*

Chapter One

Introduction

General Introduction

Among the Romantic poets, Byron is the one most known for his rebellious character, which causes him to devote himself to liberty and ideal freedom. Due to his dislike of hypocritical society of England, he chose to exile abroad where he got many inspirations to create his works. The more places he visits, the more inspirations he obtains through traveling. Byron's revolutionary fervor is conveyed through his works in his journey around the world, and his influence of satiric power against oppression is pervasive in Europe. Byron also encounters a variety of love affairs during every trip, which demonstrates a kind of erotic freedom of love. In light of this, love and freedom affect Byron's life a lot. Likewise, he puts his desire for liberty in his works, later devoting himself to fighting for independence for Greece. Paul Graham Trueblood mentions that "Byron became in the nineteenth century the 'triumpet voice of Liberty' and the acknowledged champion of Freedom" (Trueblood, *Lord Byron* 157). Thus, it is not surprising that Byron gradually reveals his idea of liberty in his works. *Don Juan* can firmly be seen as Byron's masterpiece in which we find his views on love, women, war, death, and liberal thinking. Through these multiple issues, Byron conveys the actual passions in human beings' feelings. Meanwhile, we can see that his personal views are beyond any limitations. The digressive organizations reflect his capricious personality that has transcended the constricts of both society and literary conventions. Like Juan's constant journey, everything is filled with new opportunities and not fixed. Similarly, women's conditions are also full of possibilities to develop their identities and maturity. Women do not have to be seen as a subordinate role to men in loving relations. Thus, the ironical delineation of women in the poem is actually a sincere admiration for their brave quest for love and erotic freedom. This is Byron's real-longed thinking toward human beings' freedom in love and mutual relations.

Through Byron's usage of comic and ironic style, his "mobility" [1] and personal views are quite obvious in the poem. The total effect of Byron's "mobility" is not a pattern but a kaleidoscopic way of narration. In my opinion, this kind of rhetoric is related to the ceaselessly-happened love in Juan's adventures: no limitation and boundaries. In fact, we can sense that Byron creates three distinct narrators: Juan, the narrator, and Byron himself. Juan is the protagonist whose speaking

1 Byron defines 'mobility' in a note while describing Adeline's character in the poem: "It may be defined as an excessive susceptibility of immediate impressions—at the same time without losing the past; and is, though sometimes apparently useful to the possessor, a most painful and unhappy attribute." In this point, Byron's rhetorical technique in *Don Juan* is different from other Romantic poets because of its mobile writing mode.

shows his being dominated by women's love. The narrator's view of women-Juan love relationships is objective. As to Byron the poet, he suggests his own views in the narrative. Thus, we not only know the expression on the surface but also realize Byron's own experiences as well as ideas. In my opinion, Byron's "mobility" is his percepts toward human beings, things, or ancient disciplines in *Don Juan*. His continually shifting tone in the poem makes us feel his chameleon personality reflected in his work and the traveling-like digressions for conveying his egalitarian thinking about love and both sexes. As M. H. Abrams says in *The Mirror and the Lamp*[2]: "A work of art is essentially the internal made external, resulting from a creative process operating under the impulse of feeling, and embodying the combined product of the poet's perceptions, thoughts, and feelings" (22). Byron indeed shows his thoughts and feelings by means of revising the traditional regulations or disorders which fail to reach freedom.

Though judging the familiar objects, he also does not make things lose their original quality, but revises them in a special way, like satire. This is Byron's personal vision and imagination toward things. For example, he talks about love and female sexuality with different topics without losing the original

---

2 *The Mirror and the Lamp: Romantic Theory and the Critical Tradition*, written by M.H. Abrams, is abbreviated as *The Mirror and the Lamp* in this book.

meaning of the past. In other words, he gives their balance in the quality of mobility. Under the unfixed opinions lies the most profound meaning. He does not totally refuse the previous morals on women. Instead, he conveys that women need to shatter the old confinement to reach their free-will fulfillments. This is also Byron's basic liberal thinking toward human beings. The form of *Don Juan* also contributes to the idea of liberty and non-restriction which Byron strives to achieve in his life. Viewed in this way, Byron's *Don Juan* is inherited form the Don Juan legend, but he portrays Juan as an innocent person being seduced. As in the Don Juan myth, though the theme is still about love, Byron' main purpose is to talk about people's natural emotional instincts. Only by knowing the truly inner voices can people realize what they really want. Based on Byron's ideal concept of equality, men and women share the same opportunity on their ways to love. In order to depict the admiration of female sexuality, Byron uses satire and digressions to illustrate the realistic aspect, which is even applicable to current societies—women can be independent in their decisions toward love and more sophisticated in their subjectivities. Besides, Byron's *Don Juan* is mixed with the theme of love seduction, which is similar to the Don Juan legend, but he adapts the past content to the present idea of love relations between both sexes, attempting to giving men and women a more balanced relationship. Therefore, the conventional thinking toward women and love is revised by means of Byron's satire, which assumes a quite different shape to the older myth of discipline for male/female order.

Since I mention earlier that Byron's *Don Juan* can be seen as a revolutionary work to scrutinize the relation between women and love, this poem differs greatly from the conventional Don Juan legend. The Don Juan stereotype emerged from the Spanish myth first and then was adapted into many versions. In the original Spanish tragedy, Don Juan is portrayed as an evil figure who not only seduces innocent ladies but also refuses to repent at the last minute. The Don Juan story also inspired Mozart to create the great opera "Don Giovanni" (1787). Though Mozart's work is a great music, his protagonist extremely represents the main theme of love and seduction through vocal lines. Like the conventional Don Juan legend, Mozart's Don Govanni is a love predator who entraps charming women as possible. Mozart makes sure that Don Giovanni sounds as he should be: bold, cocky, and charming. Thinking of women and lust are necessary for his life, Don Giovanni ceaselessly seduces women and even challenges the murdered stature-like ghost. The statue even gives Don Giovanni chances to repent; however, Giovanni at last goes to hell because of his strong refusal to do it. In this opera, the formation of Juan figure is not excluded from the idea of love predator. In addition to a musical version of the Don Juan legend, the Juan story was also adapted as plays, like Jose Zorrilla's *Don Juan Tenorio* (1844) and George Bernard Shaw's drama *Man and Superman* (1903). In Zorilla's version, Don Juan is saved by the virtuous Dona, for he repents his sins. And in Shaw's *Man and Superman*, one of the famous acts of the play is "Don Juan in Hell." This act focuses on the protagonist's becoming an austere and a social reformer after giving up his former career as a womanizer. What is important in the play is Shaw's idea of the "life force," which drives women to make efforts to pursue a mate in order to produce a superman after restless attempts and ceaseless quest for perfection. In this point, women's active pursuit for their love is to create a perfect person who works hard to contribute to the society. And a woman's sexual nature is a kind of allurement for attracting her lover to fall into the trap in the "life force" that she exudes. From my perspective, this love relation is established owing to the female's sacrifice to create an ideal strong-minded person. However, Shaw's adaptation senses that women's independence is on the rise, and they can take action in the love relationship which is different from the conventional masculine/feminine position.

As to Byron's *Don Juan*, the handsome Juan is also a passive role in love relationships between women; the only difference from Zorrilla's and Shaw's plays is that the female figures' active pursuit of love is to build their self-independence and individualities through various bodily performances and boundless loving energies. Unlike the Don Juan story found in earlier versions, Byron's hero is not a calculating and manipulative man, but an innocent victim whose instincts toward love are aroused by those women. Nonetheless, Byron's arrangement of Juan's journey of love is to convey the possibilities and the freedom of choice in love. Love is not involved with hierarchy, race, age and other social struggles; instead, it is worth cherishing because it gives one a new experience of knowing self through the other person. Thus, Byron represents his egalitarian thinking of human equality. In other words, not only men but also women are able to enjoy the pleasure of pursuing their lovers and happiness. In terms of conventional morality, Byron's concept of women is not subject to the old disciplines, such as "docility" and "chastity." However, he wants to tell us that love with freedom is true love. If both men and women accept the limitless chances of love, they can own their experiences of love and strengthen their maturity in the love relationships.

Based on equality and human beings' natural erotic instincts, the problem of female sexuality should be carefully scrutinized. In Byron's *Don Juan*, female sexualities include their sexual desires, emotional fulfillments, independent thinking, sympathetic behaviors, and even jealousy. That is to say, what Byron wants to show us is the various aspects of women's inner emotions toward love instead of merely focusing on the physical sex. Also, the ironic depiction of women is different from the traditional myth. Byron's technique of ottava rima rhyme scheme produces a special mode of narrative, which makes *Don Juan* one of the most influential works in English literature. And Byron's breakthrough of the form and the Don Juan story indeed create a brand new respect toward the female issues about love and freedom. Once human beings fall in love, they have equal rights to enjoy the fulfillments in love, even though in pain. The satire used in this poem is exactly Byron's critical insights toward his ideal love relation between both sexes. From women's active quest for love, we know that Byron anticipates a balanced relation between two genders and encourages them to seize the time to love in a positive way. Hence, women no longer play a weaker role in the gender system; instead, they are given a subversive energy to win their ideal lover and build self-independence and maturity. Byron's *Don Juan* is such a work that represents women's issue and love in a digressive description in which we find women gradually realize their self-consciousness in the quest for love. And Byron's admiration for human beings' passionate emotions can also be seen clearly from his depictions of women-Juan relations.

Women and Erotic Love

"Man's love is of man's life a thing apart, 'Tis woman's whole existence" is a famous quote from Byron's *Don Juan*. It is clear that Byron's love affairs occupied most of his life; moreover, such abundant love feelings inspired him to create a variety of romantic works in which women played a crucial role. *Don Juan* not only shows colorful romances but also reveals women's desires and sexualities in a positive way. This book is a representation of how women become more individualized and sophisticated through their active pursuit of love in *Don Juan*. Meanwhile, the inherent tensions of the satiric tones are the narrator's rhetorical means of compelling readers to see reality from different perspectives. Within a larger framework of satire, the issue of female sexuality and the concept of love are easily viewed in a negative way. However, Byron's usage of a comic tone does not satirize women; instead, he describes how wonderful love is in the world through images of women in love and the emotions that are the original desires of human beings. Love is the spiritual enrichment of one's daily life and a kind of symbol of energy and happiness. In addition, the author presents women's gradual getting rid of social constraints and developing their confidence. Their experiences of love offer unlimited possibilities for shaping their own identities and result in a kind of spiritual transcendence from which the new thinking and life meanings are generated.

What Byron would like to show in *Don Juan* is the exploration of human feelings, especially human passions and the nature of love. The traditional orthodoxy teaches women to follow the patriarchal rule and be chaste and obedient. In the Enlightenment, Rousseau even regards sex and pursuit of love as an irrational behavior. Until the British Romantic period, Byron thinks that it's time to change the conservative concepts of women and reveal his attitude toward women and love. As a male author, Byron can create a poem in which women become the target, so he skillfully mentions women's inner voices by transforming his male position to a female stance. Byron's rebellion against despotism is clear here in that he talks about women through a male's point of view and combines his implicit approval of romantic imagination of women in *Don Juan*. Therefore, we can see not only his ideas about women's pursuit of love and freedom of female sexuality but also his admiration for passionate love itself. Also, this is conducive for us to see women issues and realize women's minds through different angles.

The author also presents that women are gradually getting rid of social constraints and developing their confidence. Their experiences of love offer unlimited possibilities for shaping their own identities and result in a kind of spiritual transcendence from which the new thinking and life meanings are generated. In Canto I, Byron depicts Juan's hometown as "a pleasant city, / Famous for oranges and women—he / Who has not seen it will be much to pity" (I. 8. 1-3). This foreshadows a kind of romantic love which seems to appear soon. Byron knows the transience of life in this world, so he admires love so much and thinks that human beings should cherish their time to seek happiness. Though knowledge and fortune are precious things which are worth keeping, Byron still admires the treasure of love:

> But sweeter still than this, than these, than all,
> Is first and passionate love — it stands alone,
> Like Adam's recollection of his fall;
> The tree of knowledge has been pluck'd — all's known —
> And life yields nothing further to recall
> Worthy of this ambrosial sin, so shown,
> No doubt in fable, as the unforgiven
> Fire which Prometheus filch'd for us from Heaven. (I. 127. 1-8)

From the reference in the Bible, Adam and Eve are banished from Eden due to their eating of the forbidden fruit. Such a historical myth of Fall, the separation of man from God by sin, is transformed into a different shape in Romantic terms. What corresponds to the older myth of a lost paradise of Eden is now "a sense of an original identity between the individual man and nature which has been lost" (Frye 17). In Byron's view, the Fall of Adam is not a sin but a sweet Fall, like felix culpa, which is not a mistake but a key to opening the doors of knowledge of life, necessitating the redemption insured the possibility of salvation. Here women's active seeking for love reflects not only the "carpe diem" theme but also their independent minds to choose their happiness. Thus, we clearly find that Byron's attitudes toward love and sexual issues are positive, especially human beings' passions and natural love desires.

Critical Review

Since Byron's Juan is seduced, we can see the female figures are active in their pursuit of love. As the story progresses, Don Juan encounters a variety of women, such as the seductive Julia, the innocent Haidee, the powerful Gualbeyaz, the devouring Catherine, and the ideal Aurora Raby. In these love affairs, William H. Marshall observes that "[t]he identity of Juan is insubstantial and he himself is essentially passive, the victim or instrument of persons and situations in all that he encounters" (176). Therefore, we can generally realize the panoramic view of the whole poem: "the imperfection in Man's powers" (Marshall 177). This point attracts me a lot, making me want to explore more truth Byron offers in *Don Juan*. I firmly believe Byron, as a male author, reveals more female inner voices through his male stance and concept than those did by women writers. If we only seek the way and hope in women's writings, we will probably lack the balanced situations in dealing with women's issues of both sexes, like gender difference and natural sexual instincts. Thus, this is my motivation for choosing the male author's work, Byron's *Don Juan*, as my analyzing target to see the relation between women and love.

Not only is his poetry involved with female images, but Byron's life is also filled with amorous love and lovely women. Although romantic relationships can also hurt Byron, he still desires women's love and comfort with happiness. For example, he writes to his half-sister, Augusta: "Write to me Soon, my Dear Augusta, And do not forget to love me" (*Byron: A Self-Portrait*. Volume 1. 6). Byron also went through unsmooth love experiences and marriage; thus, what he desires is a fair treatment between both sexes. From the incestuous relationship with Augusta, we see that Byron does not care the racial problem between them. It is inferred that Byron's true faith in love lies in the passionate heart and devotion in a real way, not in the external obstacles or hypocrisy which handicap human beings' pursuit of love. In *Don Juan*, Byron depicts women's sexualities and his imaginative ideal love in a satirical way, which is different from other romantic poets' works, due to his influence from the neo-classical thinking. This is why we can easily see the ironic tone used in *Don Juan*. Byron indeed inherits most Pope's writing style and uses satire to connote his thinking in the poem. The different point from Pope is his usage of ottava rima, which allows the poet to build up tensions and then suddenly shifts the tone between sestet and couplet. Byron the satirist uses the Italian ottava rima to create a cynical tone that is indifferent to forms, conventions, and classes. Viewed in this way, his liberal concept is also reflected in his free style of writing. However, with the changes that take place in time and space, the unchangeable thing is Byron's liberal thinking for people—to show personal passions in a real way; thereby, women can fulfill their desires in a balanced gender code.

Even though Byron adopts Alexander Pope's style of satire in *Don Juan*, his intention of feminist depiction is not to sneer at women but to admire women's brave pursuit of love. Byron skillfully uses a digressive writing technique and even digressive events to talk about sexual topics and expand his idea of liberty further, including women's sexual aspirations. Of course, the various narrators—Byron the poet, the narrative person, and Don Juan, all play a vital role in the mobility-based depictions of female issues. According to Camille Paglia, "[t]here are heroic rescues, then capture, humiliation, and recovery, Byron ritualistically elaborates each stage of assertion and passivity, making the narrative a slow masque of sexual personae" (349). In other words, we see his depictions of amorousness and implication of love in many themes, for example, the war episode, shipwreck, or the horrible ghost canto. Upon sentimental and love issues from these events, Byron also more or less suggests his personal love affairs in *Don Juan*. Implicit is that he loves women and enjoys the deep delight from the experiences of love. Likewise, women can also enjoy the mutual treatment in love and let men devote much to their love. After all, love requires perfectly mutual trust and equality. In the poem, Byron still expresses his deep sympathy for women who either are trapped in the prison of marriage or suffer from the extreme loneliness due to the lack of love. Thus, *Don Juan* helps Byron illustrate these views about love and women.

In Chapter Two, I talk about the discourse of love and its relation between female sexuality. This chapter scrutinizes Byron's intention by focusing on female characters in his *Don Juan*. My concern here is to illustrate the positive aspect of females' active pursuit of love and show their desires, thoughts, personal will and actions. Besides, Byron arranges two reversals of gender roles: Juan as a woman in the Turkish episode, and Fitz-Fulke dressed as a ghost to pretend being a friar. The cross-dressing and reversals of both sexes symbolize a departure from the traditional binary opposition of male/female. Thus, women are not always seen as a secondary role in the gender relation. Since we know there is a natural gender difference between both sexes, the degree of their devotion to love is no exception: females have been considered more emotional than men; men regard love just as one portion of their lives. When it comes to the equality of biological sex and gender, there may be a far cry from the ideal expectation due to the traditional discipline about women's chastity or men's chauvinistic thinking. Nonetheless, Byron senses the female independence can be more and more on the way to the equality. Even though women cannot get equal treatment in biologically sexual erotics, they still can build their confidence and personal recognition through their erotic individualities—the active pursuit of the ideal love, the display of feminine traits, and so forth. In the poem, Byron expresses the idea of emancipation and freedom of female sexuality not only through women's energetic pursuit of love but also through the cross-dressing skills. In this light, we can clearly understand the connotation about the relations between gender difference and erotic equality in the perspective of Byron's arrangement of the opposition of gender roles. For instance, after drifting to Turkey and being sold as a slave, Juan is forced to prim himself as a woman 'Juanna' under Baba's order. This act of cross-dressing equals to the practice of transvestism. The adoption of transvestite undoubtedly subverts the original hierarchy of gender definition because the binary distinction of male/female is not fixed; instead, one's gender is performative. As Judith Butler in her *Gender Trouble*[3] asserts: "Gender is the repeated stylization of the body, a set of repeated acts within a highly rigid regulatory frame that congeal over rime to produce the appearance of substance, of a natural sort of being" (33). Hence, the conventional relationship between both sexes can be changed through the perfomative speech or act. This kind of performative appearance results in an attack on traditional definition of gender and sexuality, constituting a kind of subversive power to orthodoxy. Butler also contends that:

> Gender ought not to be construed as a stable identity or locus of agency from which various acts follow; rather, gender is an identity tenuously constituted in time ... must be understood as the mundane way in which bodily gestures, movements, and styles of various kinds constitute the illusion of an abiding gendered self. (140)

In Butler's view, gender is performed but not natural. If we inspect Juan's behavior in the harem, we can find Juan's

3 Butler's *Gender Trouble: Feminism and the Subversion of Identity* is abbreviated as *Gender Trouble* in this book.

difference is scarcely apparent: “His youth and features favour’d the disguise” (V. 115. 1) and “no one doubted on the whole, that she / Was what her dress bespoke” (VI. 36. 1-2). Byron’s adoption of Juan’s cross-dressing includes not only the representation of women’s oppression but also the violation of manhood. In other words, Juan’s appearance makes him become a female concubine of the sultana, receiving the long-time regulation of sex in the Eastern harem. Though Juan refuses and talks to his purchaser: “Oh, gentleman, I’m not a lady” (V. 73. 8), he still finds that he is not so much un unsesxed man as a newly powerful woman. “Juanna” thus immediately becomes the center of attention in the harem. Being a phallic woman in the harem, Juan is newly empowered by his female masquerade:

> “The prisoned eagle will not pair, nor I
> Serve a sultana’s sensual phantasy.” (V. 126. 7-8)
>
> I am not dazzled by this splendid roof;
> Whate’er thy power, and great it seems to be,
> Heads bow, knees bend, eyes watch around a throne,
> And hands obey— our hearts are still our own. (V. 127. 5-8)

In fact, it is necessary to look underneath Juan’s clothes: his repudiation for the sultana’s love represents the opposition to the dualism inherent in western thought—the male/female, or reason/emotion split that could only produce the repression and exploitation of the Other. After all, love which involves the tyrannical force and hierarchy cannot be true love. Although men and women have natural sexual difference, their erotic desires should not be measured with bias. That is to say, women are not subject to a projection or subordination for male fantasy.

As I analyze female sexuality and its relation with Juan, I indeed sense a kind of gradual emergence of subversive energy. Whenever Juan travels to different countries, he is chased by different types of women. Chapter Three examines the relation between sexuality of love and traveling in terms of Julia Kristeva's discussion of strangers and love in *Strangers to Ourselves*. For the female figures depicted in the poem, Juan becomes a foreigner to them with whom they can recognize themselves. The women-Juan affairs actually can be seen as a mother-son relationship which Kristeva defines as "chora." Thereby, women gradually reveal their subversive powers to counter patriarchal regulation. From this point of view, the female figures' aspirations of love in *Don Juan* can be considered rational. Such an ambiguous space "chora" is Kristeva's main concept of a horribly subversive power. Kristeva speaks of "the instability of the Symbolic function in its most significant aspect—the prohibition placed on the maternal body.

Here I shall name, after Plato, a chora, a receptacle" (*Powers of Horror* 14). In the process, one's ego is involved with an object in order to establish both of their identities. Kristeva further explains that there is an excessive desire, a two-way power struggle existing in the "chora" space: "[t]he conflicts of drives muddle its bed, cloud its water, and bring forth everything that, by not becoming integrated with a given system of signs, is abjection for it" (*Powers of Horror* 14). Thus, there are two seemingly contradictory powers in this "abjecting" process: On the one hand, one longs for a relation with the Other; on the other hand, one rejects and resists the Other. In this point, Kristeva says:

> The abject is the violence of mourning for an "object" that has always already been lost. The abject shatters the wall of repression and its judgments. It takes the ego back to its source on the abominable limits ... transforms death drive into a start of life, of new significance. (*Powers of Horror* 15)

Indeed, Kristeva's strange "chora" complements Freud's aspect of maternity and Lacan's symbolic order. Under the patriarchal symbol, the role of mother is oppressed because of her lack of phallus and thus being excluded from the symbolic order. However, the feminine space "chora" is mysterious and unspeakable, representing the marginality in the semiotic world.

This chaotic feminine space makes a room for the role of mother who is negative and ignored in the Symbolic order. Thus, the 'abject' condition in fact is a kind of recognition to the lack—the repressed feminine space. In other words, even though the infant enters into the Symbolic order through the abjection with his mother, he is still in the condition of feminine space where he gets the protection. And the feminine space will not disappear; instead, such feminine space is just oppressed in the unconsciousness and becoming a sort of subversive power in the patriarchal symbolic order.

From the point of Kristeva's "chora" and the abjection of self, the women-Juan relations just echo such theory of feminine space in which there is a potential deconstructing energy to patriarchy. In the poem, every woman Juan encounters basically bears her feminine quality and gradually shows a sort of subversive energy through her behaviors and bodily performances. While they face such a charming guy, their oppressed unconsciousness are induced and explored more and more. Juan, as a subject in "chora" space, experiences such an abjection process before recognizing it with the patriarchal symbol. As for these female figures, they accept the new stranger; meanwhile, they experience the abjection and counter against such an exotic subject because they still struggle with the unknown subject which seems to be an unspeakable part of themselves. Nonetheless, their extreme appreciation for Juan breaks the border of the distance between object-subject relations. For these female characters, Juan is a stranger and a seeming son who they want to protect due to their maternal instincts. They rise above their unhappiness or oppression through their contact with Juan. Also, their female sexualities are rising. Thus, the abject is a necessary process for them to recognize themselves. Kristeva further explains the concept of the foreigner as follows:

> Foreigner: a choked up rage deep down in my throat, a black angel clouding transparency, opaque, unfathomable spur.... Strangely, the foreigner lives within us: he is the hidden face of our identity, the space that wrecks our abode, the time in which understanding and affinity founder. By recognizing him within ourselves, we are spared detesting him in himself. (*Strangers* 1)[4]

The above mention means that a person may feel unease in dealing with the stranger, but he may also recognize himself more through contacting the stranger. Hence, to fit this idea in *Don Juan*, the female figures' dissatisfaction from marriage or oppression of love are evoked from Juan, an exotic stranger

4 Kristeva's *Strangers to Ourselves* is abbreviated as *Strangers* in this book.

who signals that he is "in addition." In his passivity, Juan actually falls into a series of romantic situations at each country: he attracts various dominant women—Julia, Haidee, the "imperious" Gulbeyaz, the "devouring" Catherine, the "full-blown" Fitz-Fulke, and Adeline, "The fair most fatal Juan ever met" (XIII. 12. 3). Their relations between Juan are just ambiguous because these potentially deadly women are like mother and lover at the same time. Nonetheless, Byron's intention is that women develop their own identities through such an ambiguous role—mother or lover. Under such a strong erotic power, Juan cannot resist the fusion of these females' love, just like an infant who cannot separate her mother's maternal love.

In conclusion, from the analysis of female sexuality in the discourse of love and the concept of "chora," which symbolize women's subversive power in their quest for love, we can sense that Byron admires females' exaltation of their sentimental passions and individual subjectivities in love. Besides the mother-son relationships analyzed from Kristeva's points of view, Byron's portrayal of women's active performances of their sexualities can be seen as a kind of erotic power which can create sublimity and beauty in the quest of love, so Byron reveals his ideal love situation and imagination of happiness in the poem. Love is a desire of beauty and a feeling of sublime.

And Byron's depiction of sexual passion and wonderful love just echoes Edmund Burke's aesthetic philosophy: sublime and beauty. According to Burke, the sublime is "productive of the strongest emotion which the mind is capable of feeling" (36), and the beauty is of "that quality or those qualities in bodies by which they cause love, or some passion similar to it" (83). These features are exactly the depictions of Juan and those female characters. The only distinction in this love paradise is that Juan is a receiver of love, and women are active pursuers. Moreover, Burke asserts that pain and fear "consist in an unnatural tension of the nerves" (119); these could be "qualified to cause terror" (119) and are also "a foundation capable of the sublime" (119). As a victim of love, Juan can feel such an uncomfortable feeling. In Juan's journey, the tyrannical Gulbeyaz, the despotic Catherine, and the weird Filtz Dutchess all make him feel unease. However, these female figures just broaden their new horizons through actively showing their passions to their ideal lover. Through this point of view, both Juan and these female figures all experience a kind of unprecedented impact that love brings to them.

In short, love comes with pleasure and pain, but these special experiences bring lovers new challenges and realizations toward each other. *Don Juan* indeed offers a revolutionary chance for women to notice their circumstances and cherish the opportunity of love. From the delineations of amorous atmosphere and models of female sexuality in their quest for love, we could understand that a kind of life permeated with love is totally not a waste to a healthy human being. Byron tries to tell readers that seizing the time to love is very important. Especially as a woman, she should bravely chase her happiness regardless of gender, class, race, and other oppressive elements because love is a kind of strong feeling which happens in a sudden moment without reasons or explanations. At last, Byron's attitude toward love echoes the typical thinking of Romanticism—"Sentimental emotion is over everything"—the strength and extreme value of love can save both men and women. Therefore, true freedom and fulfillment for women do contribute to equality between men and women.

Lost

I am not alone.
I know,
it is not only the matter of
inquiry but also a craving.

However, it is not a demand.
These are concerns about
needing, praying, requesting,
and the most sincere
imploring.

—— *Cheng-Fen Chen*

Chapter Two

Female Erotics

Introduction

Contradicting the supposed male aspect promised by the title *Don Juan*, Byron intentionally inspires readers with a variety of female characterization and portrayal of female sexuality in the Romantic era. Under the Romanticism permeated with imagination, emotion, and freedom, Byron's *Don Juan* totally reveals human beings' naturally attracting to beauty and love. In this poem, Byron adapts the Spanish legend *Don Juan* by making the protagonist Juan as a victim of love object and females as predators.[1] In this point of view, Byron's denial of war and his independent impulse would also be expressed while fictionizing the framework of this poem. Since the influence of Enlightenment, the rational thinking more and more becomes a standard of morality, including sexual politics. Byron thinks that such a conventional sexual morality is supposed to be reconsidered in a post-revolutionary period. This book examines Byron's *Don Juan* which represents that females gradually disregard the original sexual orthodoxy and cherish the chances of grasping their ideal loving happiness instead. Owning to the cynical tone in this poem, many critics

---

1 According to Franklin, from the beginning Byron envisaged a specifically new version of the Don Juan myth as a sexual satire, and that the setting of the story at the time of French Revolution shows his conscious decision to link sexual mores with strategies of government (*Byron's Heroines* 102).

like Wollstonecraft and Franklin mistake Byron as a misogynist. Actually, what Byron intends to do in this poem is to convey the true meaning of love for women and the positive powers of their active pursuit for love. In a word, *Don Juan* can be seen as Byron's making voice for women and attacking on the notion of propagating an ideal of chaste femininity in society.

This chapter will concentrate upon female's erotic power and sexuality in *Don Juan*. In this poem, we can see various types of female characters, including the harsh Inez, the passionate Haidee, and the imperious Gulbeyaz, to name a few. Though they show their quest for love in different ways, they bear the same characteristic—the active chasing of their desired love with positive attitudes. In light of this, all the females clearly know what they really want when facing their ideal love even they are subject to the influences of their genders and classes. And their quest for love is performed in various styles; however, these forms of pursuing love are all related to "sexuality," which is constructed by social and cultural influence. That is to say, the issue of sexuality not only refers to biological sex but also involves other aspects of sexual desires. While examining the performances of these female characters, we see they gradually establish their identities without sticking to the outside restrictions and surrounding limits.

As a romantic poet, Byron was influenced by Pope and

adopted the traditional satire to write this poem in which we can see the social truth Byron wants to reveal and his practical insight. Thus, while talking about the quest for love, Byron still adds other events and anterior allusions to depict the real intention he makes for women. In real life, Byron's personal affairs somewhat inspired him to create his writing, so it is not hard for us to imagine the women-Juan relationships are related to his own love experiences. Harold Bloom ever says that "Byron is establishing his personal or dramatized self, the satirical mask in which he will present himself as narrator of *Don Juan*" ("Introduction" 18). Byron also mentions that "I want a hero" (I. 1. 1), and there is another narrator in this poem. The narrator uses a funny tone to describe things and changes talking topics rapidly; that is to say, the narrative point of view is not fixed but full of mobility. Through such a multi-angled aspect, Byron's textual strategy makes the underlying power of the poem as a creative energy to subvert the traditional phallocentric thinking and echos with Mikhail Bakhtin's idea of carnival literature—"[l]iterature that was influenced directly and without mediation, or indirectly, through a series of indeterminate links—by one or another variant of carnivalistic folklore (ancient or medieval) we shall call carnivalized literature" (qtd. in Martin 104). Such multiple delineations can be rhetoric digressive and signal a kind of resistance to the socially powerful manipulation. Similarly, female sexuality depicted in this poem is just like such a subversive agency that cannot be regulated clearly through social limits or cultural influences.

From the western canon of literature, most male writers always shape female figures as perfect and wonderful. These women are depicted as mild and tender; other accompanied criticisms and representation of female images are basically involved with this traditional standard—woman as a passively docile weaker. In Romanticism, though the issues of women are respected more and more, most male writers tend to delineate women as a silenced figure that is beautiful as well as innocent. Only Byron bears a different attitude and insight toward women. In is easy to see that Byron makes mockery of women as jealous, tyrannical and licentious in love. Byron even ends a female figure's death in the poem: the pure Haidee must pay for her rash error in love. However, Byron still wants to "change this theme which grows too sad" (IV. 74. 1). This special rhetoric conveys that a kind of revolutionary spirit emerges: one is to subvert the conservative regulations and rules from past to the current society; the other is to deconstruct the female stereotypes created from the original doctrines.

According to Foucault, our current concept of sexuality is constructed two hundred years ago. From Foucault's point of view, human beings should critically examine the ideas of masculinity, femininity, motherhood, fatherhood, and childhood. In fact, these qualities we take for granted are all involved with underlying power struggles, knowledge, and personal ideology. Foucault also mentions that "[t]hese power mechanisms are, at least in part, those that, beginning in the eighteenth century, took charge of men's existence, men as living bodies" (*The History of Sexuality.* Volume 1. 89)[2]. In this point of view, every definition relative to sex and sexuality is established in terms of a historical form and based on phallocentric thinking. However, can such Foucaultian powerful discourse be firmly stable? Besides, Foucault mentions power exists in one's subjectivity and is a kind of discipling power which produces an ideal desire of sexuality: "docile bodies." In Foucault's point of view, the "docile bodies" of modernity in *Discipline and Punish*[3] are as follows: "The historical moment of the disciplines was the moment when an art of the human body was born … but at the

---

2 My purpose in using Foucault's concept in *The History of Sexuality* is not to mention where his position favors male or female thinking, but to point out the condition of sexual repression that existed at an earlier time. The usual theme is that women are taught to be loyal to his husband and family. Once she feels unhappy, she still needs to obey the female ethics. Even women who fulfill their desires will be seen as hysterical or irrational. Viewed in this way, Byron's insights in *Don Juan* transform female sexuality from passive restriction to active virtue. Under the ironic tone lies the real admiration for female erotics. Women's moods and behaviors are undulating with their love, which gives them more self-realization with the foreigner Juan.

3 *Foucault's Discipline and Punish: The Birth of the Prison* is abbreviated as *Discipline and Punish* in this book.

formation of a relation that in the mechanism itself makes it more obedient as it becomes more useful, and conversely" (138) and "discipline produces subjected and practiced bodies, 'docile' bodies" (138). In a word, the historical concept of human bodies is subject to the disciplines that set punishment and surveillance to the disobedient people. Nevertheless, the question is that whether the main discourse of being docile and controlled fits into the multi-vocal field of "sexuality" or not. Byron's *Don Juan* proves this point—the power of the erotic, especially female sexuality, is still exalted to free herself from the serious regulations and subvert the confinement of social rules, even being able to deconstruct the masculine/feminine power relation. In Byron's *Don Juan*, we can find implicitly female sexualities gradually develop their won ways and are involved with subversive energy to resist the mainstream argument about sexual discourse.

Don Juan can be seen as a work in which women release their sexualities; that is, women's love desires are satisfied. According to Stevi Jackson, "[s]exuality cannot be understood [as] if it is separated from [...] such things as the relations between the sexes, the cultural ideas of 'love', or the institution of marriage. Sexual behavior is social behavior; it is not just the consummation of some biological drive" (62). In this poem, all the females' behaviors echo the above definition; these female characters chase their love because of not only the biological drives but also the social factors, values, attitudes, and behaviors in which female sexuality may be better understood. Female's sexual desire has been oppressed by patriarchal powers and marital restriction for a long time. Under such regulation, women become inferior and dependent, even losing the pleasure of seeking for true love. Byron, who bears a capricious personality and devotes much attention to independence, just rips the veil of such a hypocritical male/female ethics by showing female subversive sexuality in *Don Juan*. Thus, both the non-linear narrative structure and the women's sexual energy in the poem offer a kind of instability and more possibilities for subversion to the fixed orthodoxy, which symbolizes women's repudiation of being restrained.

In the beginning of the poem, Byron depicts Donna Julia who is married to a man of fifty. Julia gradually knows she lost any happiness in this marriage. While finding Juan is so attractive, she cannot help falling in love with him in a short moment. Julia even cannot care about her religion and marital morality. In a word, temptation of love stills overrides interior struggles. Actually, Julia knows how to flirt with Juan in her passionate quest for love:

> Yet Julia's very coldness still was kind,

And tremulously gentle her small hand
Withdrew itself from his, but left behind
A little pressure, thrilling, and so bland
And slight, so very slight, that to the mind
'T was but a doubt; but ne'er magician's wand
Wrought change with all Armida's fairy art
Like what this light touch left on Juan's heart. (I. 71. 1-8)

Here, Byron depicts female's action for pursuing love as a powerful dominance of man. Julia's sexuality is performed with her autonomy without considering the patriarchal oppression because all she need is just the ideal love she met. In light of this, Caroline Franklin says that "[w]riting in a climate of political conservatism and evangelical fervour, Byron set his story of Don Juanism a generation back, in the revolutionary decade, perhaps suggesting that subversive sexuality now takes the place of revolution" (Franklin, *Don Juan* 84). Why such a married woman still pursues immoral love? Under what kind of circumstance could women show their erotic instincts to satisfy their sentimental desires? Byron intentionally uses female sexuality as a subversive agency to deconstruct the traditional phenomenon of male/female relationship, supporting women's quest for love. In this point, women are not like a creature which is subject to its natural sexual desire; instead, they enjoy such rapture in the process of pursuing love.

Female Sexuality and Sexual Pleasure

Women indeed get pleasure in the process of pursuing love. In this poem, Julia takes pains to win Juan's heart and even makes intrigues to cheat her husband. She feels unsafe but then enjoying such an exciting love experience regardless of God's rules. Byron describes her behavior: "... her soft lips lie apart, / And louder than her breathing beats her heart" (I. 158. 7-8). Julia experiences unprecedentedly sweet pleasure in this love affair, becoming confident and passionate more and more. Even when she faces her marital crisis, she stills cannot resist the magic of love. Besides, having her body touched by Juan, Julia's sexual desire is also satisfied:

> And Julia sate with Juan, half embraced
>   And half retiring from the glowing arm,
> Which trembled like the bosom where't was placed; (I. 115. 1-3)

> Antonia puzzled; Julia did not speak,
> But pressed her bloodless lip to Juan's cheek. (I. 169. 7-8)

> He turn'd his lip to hers, and with his hand
>   Call'd back the tangles of her wandering hair;
> Even then their love they could not all command,

> And half forgot their danger and despair:
>
> Antonia's patience now was at a stand—
>
> 'Come, come, 't is no time now for fooling there,'
>
> (I. 170. 1-6)

Julia always thinks about love and sweet happiness, so she bravely makes chances to be together with Juan. Her sexuality isn't just about bodily desire but also her inspiration about spiritual satisfaction in love. Though Julia is parted from Juan in the end, she still writes a love letter to fulfill her quest for love. All Julia does is to satisfy her perfect experiences of feminine sexuality. Just like what Irigaray says: "Her sexuality, always at least double, goes even further: it is plural" (207). Woman changes herself in body or mind through her released sexuality in the sea of love.

As Juan ends his affair with Julia, he is pushed by her mother to be on a voyage to Greece, making compensating for what he did in Spanish. Yet, Juan cannot escape the attraction of love. After a shipwreck, Juan drifts to an island where he meets a beautiful girl called Haidee. Byron depicts Haidee as a passionate heroine who bravely defends her love with Juan and resists her father's patriarchal power. Haidee's sexuality is seemingly masculine because she always takes care of Juan with her whole mind and even is willing to die for Juan. Besides, Haidee's southern Moorish blood symbolizes her natural passion for sensual love, which is an instinct that Byron wants to convey his idea of women's sexual freedom:

> ... she was one
> Made but to love, to feel that she was his
> Who was her chosen. What was said or done
> Elsewhere was nothing. She had nought to fear,
> Hope, care, nor love beyond, her heart beat here. (II. 202. 4-8)

Haidee has a crush on Juan at first sight, totally revealing her quest for Juan's love. She is not subject to the surroundings but pursues her innocent love experience. Byron's intention here shows that female sexuality is natural and should not be constrained by chastity or social morality. According to Franklin, Haidee and Juan's romantic love can be seen as "a means of personal liberation: the creation of a private enclave of freedom.... Haidee, provides a paradisal haven for Juan on her Greek isle. She acts spontaneously, not constrained by Christian morality or social considerations" (Franklin, *Byron* 83). Thus, Haidee's sexuality is expressed with her autonomy, acting like Eve who is punished for her original sin of eating forbidden fruit but is praised by Byron for her beginning of human beings' love. Haidee touches Juan's body spontaneously and feels the surrounding is filled with love between Juan and herself. For Haidee, she gets pleasure from such interaction with Juan, and her sexuality goes even further, which fits Irigaray's idea that "the sexuality is plural" (207). Byron expresses such pleasure as follows: "Round her she made an atmosphere of life, / The very air seemed lighter form her eyes" (III. 74. 1-2).

Although the author arranges a patriarchal figure, Lambro, as a powerful rule to regulate Haidee's and Juan's behaviors, Byron still makes us see the positive energy in love. That is to say, Haidee is indeed born to love and died of love at last. Love and emotion are the original desires of human beings and also the spiritual enrichment of daily lives. In Boyd's view, Juan and Haidee are "children of nature, and their love is the real, natural passion" (66). Contrasted with Lambro's violent defeat for blocking Juan and Haidee's precocious love, Haidee's determined mind for love represents a kind of spontaneous passion and positive action in this world where Byron condemns for its hypocrisy and unitary discipline of masculine and feminine ethic code. What's more, Haidee ignores the problem of race existing between Juan and her, taking pains to fulfill her love desire by showing the feminine sexuality without the constrictions of social regulation and taking the dominant role in the pleasure of seduction. The following are the lines which Byron suggested his idea of females' sexual freedom through the sexual role reversal—Juan is not a reluctant victim but vulnerable to Haidee's seduction even they cannot communicate with the same language because of their different races:

And then fair Haidee tried her tongue at speaking,
    But not a word could Juan comprehend,
Although he listened so that the young Greek in
    Her earnestness would ne'er have made an end; (II. 161. 1-4)

And now, by dint of fingers and of eyes,
    And words repeated after her, he took
A lesson in her tongue, but by surmise,
    No doubt, less of her language than her look:
As he who studies fervently the skies
    Turns oftener to the stars than to his book, (II. 163. 1-6)

He was her own, her ocean-treasure, cast
Like a rich wreck— her first love and her last. (II. 173. 7-8)

In a sense, Haidee knows what her really wants and resists the obstacles between Juan and her with efforts. Conversely, Don Juan's virility is not subject to the taming influence of love. In this love relation, Byron tells us women should seize the time to enjoy the pleasure love brings, together with capitalizing on their erotic powers to reach the area of individual liberation and self-knowledge.

In Juan-Julia and Juan-Haidee affairs, we see that Byron punishes these two women: one is sent to the nunnery, and the other who is having a little baby is dead. However, the most important implicit meaning is both they chase their love at exchange of their reputation or life. The more love they desire, the more prices they need to pay. Actually, Byron here suggests females' bravery to pursue their emotional desires regardless of the bondage of marriage or patriarchal discipline of society. In this poem, Byron mentions that "Man's love is of his life a thing apart, / 'Tis woman's whole existence ..." (I. 194. 1-2). The tone of this verse is suggested with admiring attitude of women's seizing love: love is crucial for them; even when facing difficulties, all they can do is to love again and devote much to love. Byron assigns women's ruling passions as the need to love and to be loved. Everybody is born to love and enjoy the pleasure of love. This is a sincere reflection of Byron's attitude toward love, and he also projects his idea of freedom on women. That is to say, women should live with their autonomy to show their passions and quest for love since love signifies women's whole lives. If not, women's emotions and erotic desires will be limited and pitiful. This is why Byron uses female figures as active pursuers in the seduction of Juan; Byron celebrates women's erotic love as an expression of their defiant individualism which is subversive to the constraints of social and moral law. Female sexuality thus involves a subversive power to the outer regulation of society.

Women, Byron thinks, can really love and actively express their hearts to their lovers. Byron furthers does not believe the Platonic love because such a spiritual love must result in the physical basis of life and love as well: "Oh Plato! Plato! you have paved the way, / With your confounded fantasies to more … / A charlatan, a coxcomb—and have been, / At best, no better than a go-between" (I. 116. 1-8). Namely, spiritual love is not enough for human beings to feel the true pleasure of love. Sweeter than this spiritual realization is passionate love. Just like the 'Original' sin Adam and Eve made, life yields nothing further to compare this forbidden paradise. Since time is transient, Byron tells us we should seize the time to enjoy such gift Eve made for us. Similarly, if women always obey the social law or morality, they cannot free to express their aspirations of love. It is the reason why Byron depicts a variety of women who pursue the young Juan; in a word, Byron would like to celebrate female sexuality as a subversive agency to overthrow the latent operation of social mechanism. Also, Byron's sympathy for women is as follows:

> They are right; for Man, to man so oft unjust,
>
> Is always so to Women: one sole bond
>
> Awaits them — treachery is all their trust;
>
> Taught to conceal, their bursting hearts despond

Over their idol, till some wealthier lust
    Buys them in marriage — and what rests beyond?
A thankless husband — next a faithless lover —
Then dressing, nursing, praying — and all's over. (II. 200. 1-8)

Poor Thing of Usages! coerced, compelled,
    Victim when wrong, and martyr oft when right,
Condemned to child-bed, as men for their sins
Have shaving, too, entailed upon their chins. — (XIV. 23. 5-8)

A daily plague, which in the aggregate
    May average on the whole with parturition. —
But as to women — who can penetrate
    The real sufferings of their she condition?
Man's very sympathy with their estate
    Has mush of selfishness and more suspicion.
Their love, their virtue, beauty, education,
But form good housekeepers — to breed a nation. (XIV. 24. 1-8)

His sympathy for women leads him to consider female's sexual politics. As a rebelliously Romantic individualist, "Byron attacks the notion of the state as a collection of male-headed families.... The suppression and control of the female libido by men is not a good foundation for government, for the imbalance of power fuels male aggression and leads to female manipulativeness"

(Franklin, *Byron* 101). This also explains why Byron describes Juan as a passive person and focuses instead on a lot of female characters from different countries in the poem.

As Juan is hit by Lambro and drifts to Turkey where he is sold as a slave, the sultan's wife, Gulbeyaz, sees him and orders the eunuch Baba to buy Juan immediately. Gulbeyaz lives in a harem in which there are other damsels dwell, and all of these damsels are taught to control their chastity under the oriental rules. In this Turkish episode, we see Byron discloses the sexual oppression of oriental girls who serve the powerful sultan. Yet, Byron admires the oriental passions which are "not a thing of that a stringent quality" (V. 157. 4) in the North. In Schlegel's point of view, "the Orient is the most sublime form of the Romantic" (qtd. in Franklin, *Don Juan* 75). For the human beings' erotic instincts, it is also an illicit space and affords a way of indulging sensual fantasy which is displaced as the product of an inferior civilization. The sexual adventurer, Don Juan, whose voyage into this mysterious territory rips the veil of the oriental girls' oppression: "Thus in the East they are extremely strict, / And Wedlock and a Padlock mean the same" (V. 158. 1-2). Byron's liberal thinking indeed engages with the discourses of Orientalism which is commented by Edward Said since the late 18th century:

> Orientalism can be discussed and analyzed as the corporate institution for dealing with the Orient-dealing with it by making statements about it, authorizing views of it, describing it, by teaching it, settling it, ruling over it: in short, Orientalism as a Western style for dominating, restructuring, and having authority over the Orient ... Moreover, so authoritative a position did Orientalism have that I believe no one writing, thinking, acting on the Orient could do so without taking account of the limitations on thought and action imposed by Orientalism. (qtd. in Franklin, *Don Juan* 74-75)

Here Byron tells us about Orientalism under Western values appertaining to gender and race. Women's feminine qualities are subject to patriarchal despotism. In *Don Juan*, Byron writes "Four wives and twice five hundred maids, unseen, / were ruled as calmly as a Christian queen" (V. 148. 7-8). But through Gulbeyaz's situation, we see that Gulbeyaz is a powerful woman Byron creates to denounce the discourses of Orientalism.

The Reversal of Gender Role

Byron has Juan undergo the exploitation of these inferior class, race, and sex by experiencing for himself the sexual oppression of women at its most extreme—in the sultan's harem.

Juan is bought by Baba in the slave market and is asked to dress as a woman. When Baba takes Juan to see the sultana Gulbeyaz, Baba "Motioned to Juan to approach, and then / A second time desired him to kneel down / And kiss the lady's foot …" (V. 102. 2-4). This condition implies that Gulbeyaz owns a noble status than Juan; however, Gelbeyaz actually is a frustrated wife who shared her husband with three other wives and fifteen hundred concubines. When she sees the handsome Juan on his way to the slave market, she decides to buy him and asks Juan: "Christian, canst thou love" (V. 116. 7). In doing so, she runs the risk of losing her own life. Obviously, Gulbeyaz is still eager to love because her sexual desire cannot be satisfied in this harem. Gulbeyaz is also unsure why she bears a sorrow mind; she just chases an ideal love with her power and nobility. In this poem, we can see Gulbeyaz's feminine quality is transformed to be masculine in that she manages a lot of concubines and has tyranny over Juan. According to Manning's research:

> The transformation marks the uncertain of Juan's sexual identity, and represents the collapse of masculine image Byron's heroes have struggled to preserve. In Byron's world, sexual roles are not determined by genes alone, but by power: as Juan is helpless, he becomes a woman. Concurrently, the beautiful Gulbeyaz who has purchased him becomes masculine because of her position. She

> is described as 'imperious' and self-willed, exactly like Napoleon or the heroes of Byron's tales. Like them, she commands love and treats its objects like slaves: that is, like women-hence Juanna. ("The Byronic Hero" 57)[4]

The reversal of roles contributes to Byron's intentional vision of the human beings' passions, and it is Gulbeyaz who represents the figure of passionate sexuality. Gulbeyaz actively seduces Juan with a threatening attitude, like "the sweetness of the devil" (V. 109. 2). Through demonstrating that aristocratic woman, like Gulbeyaz, is capable as a man of using sexuality in a relationship, the essentialist assumptions about gender are deconstructed.

As an oriental bride, Gulbeyaz is not submissive to the despotic regulation of sex; instead, she knows how to seduce the handsome Juan: "At length, in an Imperial way, she laid / Her hand on his and bending on him eyes, / Which needed not an empire to persuade, / Looked into his for love, where none replies" (V. 125. 1-4). However, Juan refuses her quest for love and bursts into tears to express 'feminine' sentiment. In my opinion, Juan's repudiation for Gulbeyaz is because of her powerful treatment. In terms of Byron's intention of

4 This essay "The Byronic Hero as Little Boy," written by Peter J. Manning, is abbreviated as "The Byronic Hero" in this book.

independence and freedom, female sexuality as a subversive agency is not based on a despotic way. Thus, we perceive that it is Gulbeyaz's unfeminine domination, not absence of love, which is the real stumbling block. In fact, Juan's cross-dressing as a female represents those seraglio concubines in the harem, "… a thousand and bosoms there / Beating for love as the caged birds for air" (VI. 26. 7-8). His feminine style also reveals a kind of resistance to the masculine control and a woman's positive value because her sexual rebellion against patriarchy is meaningful. When the odalisques are released from male control in their own apartments, they become wild, compared to animals, children, lunatics and the lower-class of a colonized nation:

> Like birds, or boys, or bedlamites broke loose,
> Waves at spring tide, or women anywhere
> When freed from bonds (which are of no great use
> After all), or like Irish at a fair, (VI. 34. 2-5)

The female libido is Orientalized in the suggestion that Eastern women are more libidinous by nature anyway. In Byron's view, women's sexuality should not be repressed, but instead be released owing to the fact that female sexuality is a natural instinct and is supposed to be rational, especially in the quest for love.

Even though Byron makes Juan refuse Gulbeyaz's treatment, he still establishes a theme of passion that can be found in Gulbeyaz's personality. Like Donna Julia, she wants love and cannot get it easily. Gulbeyaz's love toward Juan is so strong that she cannot accept other girls' emotions toward Juan. When she learns that Juan, as "Juanna," has shared the bed of the concubine Dudu, she resolves to destroy both of them. Actually, this is Gulbeyaz's call for the liberal rhetoric, for all she does is just to attain "his heart" (V. 140. 8). As a noble bride, Gulbeyaz lives a poor life because of the terrible marriage. In this Turkish canto, Byron reveals his sympathy for women again, renouncing the despotic control but praising the freely-expressed female sexuality identified with nature. Boyd points out that "[t]hen at Gulbeyaz's humiliated weeping, Juan automatically unbends and begins to yield" (67). At last, Gulbeyz's sexuality overcomes every obstacle in her pursuit of the passionate love. Byron not only admires the freedom of female sexuality but also suggests the idea of "carpe diem"—seize the time whenever you have the chance to love:

> But there she slept, not quite so fair to see,
>   As ere that awful period intervenes
> Which lays both men and women on the shelf,
> To mediate upon their sins and self. (VI. 69. 5-8)

Implicit in this verse is that human beings should try their best to cherish the transient lives and love. Byron hates the rules and regularity of a sentimental affair, together with those constraints on women. And Byron's view of women echoes what Beauvoir says: "One is not born, but rather becomes, a woman" (qtd. in Leitch 1403). The truth is that women are influenced by surroundings but are not naturally seen as an inferior sex. Thus, women must develop their autonomy to resist the social patriarchy.

In order to illustrate the positive aspect of females' active pursuit of love and show their desires, thoughts, personal will and actions, Byron also focuses on his female characters' bodily performances in a carnival way. In *Don Juan*, Byron arranges two reversals of gender roles: Juan as a woman in Turkish, and Fitz-Fulke dressed as a ghost to pretend being a friar. Through such a transformation of dressing, the sexual ideology is not anything fixed; instead, the cross-dressing involves a potentially deconstructing energy to oppose the despotic discourse. While looking at Juan's gender reversal, we also see Byron's depiction of the seraglio complicates the "binary logic" of masculine/ feminine discourses as well. Not only Juan's transvestite but also the black eunuch, Baba, can be a good example. Being confused by the sultana's capricious personality, Baba once celebrates himself as a "third sex" (IV. 86. 8). On the slave ship, Juan is chained to a woman captive to become a temporary androgyny, "an odd male, and odd female" (IV. 92. 2.), and Byron interestingly insists on Juan's acceptance and impotence to the request of gender reversal. In light of this, such a "phallocentric or phallotropic" principle is threatened by Juan's feminine transformation. Gradually, Byron's intention to expose the sexual difference is more apparent. Though one's sexual ideology is unchangeable, one's gender is built through social practice, not inherent. Therefore, one's sexual difference also can be changed in the discourse of sexuality.

Byron depicts the transformation in the arbitrariness of male privilege that Juan's masculinity—now "Juanna"—becomes the only phallic woman in the harem during his night in the seraglio. After being desired as a man in a woman's dress, Juan becomes the sultana's ideal lover. At the same time, being a man desired as a woman "Juanna," Juan is appreciated by Lolah, Katinka, and Dudu. In this point, Juan's masculine quality is almost gone in the harem; the war between women is going to emerge, threatening the male hegemony in such a disciplined eastern country. In addition, Byron mentions extended reference to Semiramis, "who was fabled to have ruled Assyria in her husband's clothing, history's first transvestite" (qtd. in Richardson 180). Semiramis's authority over her husband symbolizes the gradual collapse of patriarchal power. In my opinion, Byron's usage of gender reversal and transvestite-related allusions is to depict women's opposition to being a second role in gender roles. And Byron's

"Juanna" is a man who can realize women's plight by means of dressing female attire. In this way, Juan's sexual adventure will, moreover, problematize rather than reinforce his sense of phallic dominance. In other words, we can see that there are more rooms for women to share their thoughts and show their bodily performances in a positive way. The sexual stereotype is totally changed by having Juan be effeminate as a victim of love affairs with Gulbeyaz, Catherine the Great and the England Duchess Fitz-Fulke. All these three heroines all regard men as their sexual slaves, and their aggressive behaviors to seek love are a proof to show their decisive minds and establish women's authority over men. Thus, the act of reversing the traditional gender codes symbolically transgresses the normative hierarchical man-women position.

In the Ottoman sultana episode, Byron accomplishes his desire to evade the hierarchical character of contemporary gender relations by means of transvestite costume. Human society has been constituted principles of making men on top and women as a subordinate role. However, when men dress women's attire, they symbolically lose the top position in gender system. Likewise, women can also obtain their freedom and development through the masculine disguise, which enables women to overcome barriers that refrain their individualities in a feminist view. In short, Byron's adoption of cross-dressing costume challenges the conventional definitions of both sexuality and gender. Also, this potential subversion to the gender system and the struggles between two sexes are correspondent to Bakhtin's concept of carnivalization:

> Carnival is past millennia's way of sensing the world as one great communal performance. This sense of the world, liberating one from fear, bringing the world ... opposed to that one-sided and gloomy official seriousness which is dogmatic and hostile to evolution and change, which seeks to absolutize a given condition of existence or a given social order. From precisely that sort of seriousness did the carnival sense of the world liberate man. But there is not a grain of nihilism in it, nor a grain of empty frivolity or vulgar bohemian individualism. (160)

From Bakhtin's point of view, carnival is a world where there is a diversity of grotesque or unrestricted voices permeated with laughter and disruptive element, deconstructing the official culture and its regulation. In *Don Juan*, we see Juan's disguise as "Juanna" just echoes such carnival spirit, a kind of "glamorous, contradictory extension of the physical body—a capricious addition that suggested the body going beyond itself..." (Castle, *Masquerade*[5] 76). Similar with Bakhtin's idea, Castle's concept

5 *Castle's Masquerade and Civilization: The Carnivalesque in Eighteenth-Century English Culture and Fiction* is abbreviated as *Masquerade* in this

toward disguise is that "[l]ike the 'carnivalized' body of ancient festive tradition described by Bakhtin, the double body of masquerade is not a closed, complete unit; it is unfinished, outgrows itself, transgresses its own limits" (*Masquerade* 76).

The carnival spirit gives us many opportunities to inverse the normal behavior, turning every authoritative standard upside down. Hence, everything serious or hegemonic is meant to be challenged and revised. In the Turkish canto, Byron expresses the idea of emancipation and freedom of female sexuality not only through women's energetic pursuit of love but also through the cross-dressing technique. For instance, after drifting to Turkish and being sold as a slave, Juan is forced to prim himself as a woman 'Juanna' under Baba's order. This act of cross-dressing equals to the practice of carnival transvestism.

The adoption of transvestite undoubtedly subverts the original hierarchy of gender definition because the binary distinction of male/female is not fixed; instead, one's gender is performative. Butler in her *Gender Trouble* asserts: "Gender is the repeated stylization of the body, a set of repeated acts within a highly rigid regulatory frame that congeal over rime to produce the appearance of substance, of a natural sort of being" (33). Hence, the conventional relationship between both

---

book.

sexes can be changed through the performative speech or act. This kind of performative appearance results in an attack on traditional definition of gender and sexuality, constituting a kind of subversive power to orthodoxy. Butler also says that:

> Gender ought not to be construed as a stable identity or locus of agency from which various acts follow; rather, gender is an identity tenuously constituted in time, instituted in an exterior space through a stylized repetition of acts. The effect of gender is produced through the stylization of the body and, hence, must be understood as the mundane way in which bodily gestures, movements, and styles of various kinds constitute the illusion of an abiding gendered self. (140)

In Butler's view, gender is performed but not natural. If we inspect Juan's behavior in the harem, we can find Juan's difference is scarcely apparent: "His youth and features favour'd the disguise" (V. 115. 1), and "no one doubted on the whole, that she / Was what her dress bespoke ..." (VI. 36. 1-2). Byron's adoption of Juan's cross-dressing includes not only the representation of women's oppression but also the violation of manhood. In other words, Juan's appearance makes him become a female concubine of the sultana, receiving the long-time regulation of sex in the Eastern harem. Juan actually refuses to wear female attire as he talks to Baba: "Old gentleman, I'm not a lady" (V. 73. 8). However, after his masquerade arranged by Baba, Juan still finds that he is not so much an unsexed man as a newly powerful woman. "Juanna" thus immediately becomes the center of attention in the harem. Being a phallic woman in the harem, Juan feels newly empowered by his female masquerade:

> "The prisoned eagle will not pair, nor I
> Serve a sultana's sensual phantasy. (V. 126. 7-8)
>
> I am not dazzled by this splendid roof;
> Whate'er thy power, and great it seems to be,
> Heads bow, knees bend, eyes watch around a throne,
> And hands obey— our hearts are still our own." (V. 127. 5-8)

Referring to Juan's "travesty" in the harem, Wolfson points out "it is important to keep in mind that Juan's 'masquerade' is Oriental as well as feminine" (qtd. in Richardson 178). Actually, it is necessary to look underneath Juan's clothes: his repudiation for the sultana's love represents the opposition to the dualism inherent in western thought—the male/female, or reason/emotion split that could only cause the repression and exploitation of the Other. After all, love which involves the tyrannical force and hierarchy cannot be a true love. Although men and women have natural sexual difference, their erotic desires should not be measured with bias—women become a projection or subordination for male fantasy. Thus, such gender reversal in this section of Juan's cross-dressing is not simply a temporary exchange of sexual roles, but a kind of vehicle of probing more aspects about the grounds of sexual difference of both sexes.

From the above analysis of gender reversal, Byron makes a revolutionary chance that female owns a subversive power in their choice of love. Their sentimental desires or sexualities can resist the oppressive patriarchy. The cross-dressed "Juanna" is just a typical representation of such a powerful figure that is opponent to the tyrannical Gulbeyaz and discloses the pitiful situations of women in the harem. These oppressed females are just like birds which desire to fly freely, emancipating from the districted prison:

> Don Juan in his feminine disguise,
> With all the damsels in their long array,
> Had bowed themselves before the imperial eyes,
> And at the usual signal ta'en their way
> Back to their chambers, those long galleries
> In the seraglio, where the ladies lay
> Their delicate limbs, a thousand bosoms there
> Beating for love as the caged birds for air. (VI. 26. 1-8)

Here Byron points out the desire of love in every woman's heart.

Through such a transformation of gender roles, Byron's Juan breaks the border of binary male/female opposition. Under the mask of being a phallic woman, Juan sees the Oriental place as a despotic oppression for women. Byron portrays the Orient as the exotic "other," functioning as what Raymond Schwab calls the "alter-ego to the Occident" (qtd. in Richardson 183). Hence, the Turkish canto is also a reaction to the western cultural hegemony which projects the oriental world as a fantasy space for the occidental erotic/sadistic male desire. Byron points out the confinement for the women in the odalisque:

> The Turks do well to shut— at least, sometimes—
>   The women up— because, in sad reality,
> Their chastity in these unhappy climes
>   Is not a thing of that astringent quality
> Which in the North prevents precocious crimes
>   And makes our snow less pure than our morality; (V. 157. 1-6)

> Thus in the East they are extremely strict,
>   And Wedlock and a Padlock mean the same;
> Excepting only when the former's picked
>   It ne'er can be replaced in proper frame; (V. 158. 1-4)

Every country actually more or less discriminates against women due to the societal discipline. And women in the third world even suffer from the occidental values and standards. Here, Byron points out that regardless of race or blood, human beings all bear their passionate feelings and desires. Also, people have their rights to seek their happiness in their own ways. Hence Byron exposes the arbitrariness of the binary system on the different culture based on the western "phallic imperialism." Gradually, we find that the traditional forms and systems are reduced to nonsense by showing Juan's inability of being masculine and women's active pursuit of love, toghether with their subversion to the conventional binary opposition of gender system.

As the narrator goes on, Juan, dressed as Juanna, is marched to the harem with other concubines. Due to shortage of beds, Juanna is forced to sleep with the lovely Dudu. Dudu is described as a love goddess, "with massive erotic potential waiting to be aroused and capable of arousing others" (Montag 32). Juan has pity for Dudu, who is arranged as a bed partner with him. In the beginning, she is obedient and makes efforts explaining her unsolicited dream to avoid the punishment. However, Juan even helps Dudu to explain that "She did not find herself the least disposed / To quit her gentle partner and to dwell" (VI. 84. 5-6). DuDu immediately "turned round / And hid her face within Juanna's breast: / Her neck alone was seen, but that was found / The colour of a budding rose's crest"

(VI. 85. 1-4). DuDu's performance changes quickly because of Juan's words and her original appreciation of him. Within her limited area of action, she has apparently enjoyed the freedom she has. Even though being unknown to the fact that Juan is a man, Dudu still shows her sexually-erotic friendship with Juan. Here, we can be implied that Byron even accepts androgynous sex or homosexual love, which proves his intention for pursuing the freedom of love. Hence, Juan's repudiation to Gulbeyaz and DuDu's performance can be both considered a positively female power and devoted sexuality agency.

In addition to the admiration of female sexuality, Byron also satirizes the hypocrisy in high society of England. In the poem, Adeline lives in her high social circle and loves her husband, but her love for him costs her an effort. She is drawn to Juan because she finds in him a warmth that is lacking in her husband. Her courtesy toward those people who vote her husband is actually superficial; her real frustration of her strong feelings is her marriage. As a result, Adeline gradually finds her role as a devoted political and social hostess, "a dreary void" (XIV. 79. 1). As the matter of fact, there is a strong passion in her mind: "... beneath the snow, / As a volcano holds the lava more / Within ..." (XIII. 36. 2-4). That is to say, Adeline actually at heart is deeply passionate and sentimental. However, sticking to the bondage of marriage, Adeline cannot pursue her love freely. She becomes a matchmaker and prepares a loveless marriage for Juan because only by this method can she assure a room for herself in Juan's heart. Byron's intention here deplores that marriage is an awful wedlock which destroys the freedom of individuals. Adeline's behavior indeed reveals a kind of rebellion against her loveless marriage though she must still obey the aristocratic rule in high society. Moreover, Byron also satirizes the English aristocratic ladies:

> With other countesses of Blank— but rank;
>   At once the "lie" and the "elite" of crowds,
> Who pass like water filtered in a tank,
>   All purged and pious from their native clouds;
> Or paper turned to money by the Bank:
>   No matter how or why, the passport shrouds
> The passé and the *passed*; *for* good society
> Is no less famed for tolerance than piety,—(XIII. 80. 1-8)

Under such a sarcastic tone, Byron mentions the true essence of their hearts; that is, the passionate hearts and even the feelings of inferiority lurk in the innocent appearances. For Byron, the bonds or artificial courtesy should be dismantled.

In the English episode, Byron attacks the hypocritical bluestockings and their superficially social performances. The portrayal of Adeline is just a representation of the artificiality of Northern femininity. Byron thinks that her frustrated female sexuality should not be repressed but must be revealed in the pursuit of love. Byron also mentions that marriage and love are so frequently antithetical:

> 'Tis melancholy and a fearful sign
>   Of human frailty, folly, also crime,
> That love and marriage rarely can combine,
>   Although they both are born in the same clime; (III. 5. 1-4)

In light of this, marriage is thought of as the end of romantic love and even becomes a kind of bondage for women. Thus, from the beginning to the end of the poem, Byron depicts various miserable female figures trapped in the loveless marriage. In their love affairs with Juan, they all take the initiative in their respective ways, which explicitly reveals Byron's contention that female sexuality subverts the social limits and sexual orthodoxy. Although many women of the 19th English society and Wollstonecraft all emphasize the importance of a stable marriage for women, Byron denies this thinking and regards marriage as a kind of bondage which gives female no freedom to enjoy their sensual love. Therefore, romantic love becomes a passionate redemption for women to release their dominant sexualities and recognize themselves.

Since Byron conveys that love can be a kind of redemption

for saving females from becoming a subordinate role in both sexes, it is inferred that love gives women boundless energy to establish their independence and maturity. Still, Byron uses digression to describe his admiration toward love and female sexuality. His disclosure of the hypocritical English society underlies the aspired freedom of female sexuality and the female figures' aggressive powers. In the English society canto, the England Duchess Fitz-Fulke's pursuit of love comes to be the most aggressive figure. Her sexual role reversal is used to convey the deconstructing energy toward the surrounding limits that will handicap her pursuit of happiness. In order to depict Juan as a victimized lover of Duchess Fitz-Fulke, Byron also adds gothic elements in the English society. The Duchess Fitz-Fulke is also a representation of erotic desire. Living in the hypocritical British society, Fitz-Fulke acts differently from other noble ladies: she obviously shows her desire of satisfaction for sexuality in cross-dressing as a ghost. Originally, Fitz-Fulke just refrains herself from her husband's restraint and pursues her erotic pleasure through her bodily performance. As to her marriage, she also suffers from a loveless marriage because she seldom gets together with her husband. After she meets Juan, she becomes more active in pursuing her ideal happiness. In Byron's arrangement to make the Duchess pretend as a black friar, Byron again expresses the carnival representation of gender reversal. However, under the prank to be a ghost, Fitz-Fulke behaves exactly what Byron wants to convey: to show the extreme feeling of sublime in her sensual arousal and exaltation of sexuality.

Regardless of the limits of conventional morality, Fitz-Fulke manages to seduce Juan, refusing to be a so-called docile lady in the noble society. Again, Byron here points out his sympathy toward women in the marriage. If there is no love in marriage, this kind of pseudo happiness is just a waste of time. Moreover, love which isn't involved with freedom cannot be a true love. Fitz-Fulke's active behavior toward her ideal love challenges the conservative and traditional English society, disguising as a gothic friar to fulfill her sensual and amorous desires toward the handsome Juan. Her bodily performance brings a kind of subversive energy; the gothic atmosphere also evokes feelings of terror and laughter, which are all related to relief of excessive emotions. In *Don Juan*, Byron also sets a ghost story in Norman Abbey, thereby depicting an imaginative picturesque mansion of amorous exaltation among the gothic ambiences:

> Amidst the court a Gothic fountain play'd,
>   Symmetrical, but deck'd with carvings quaint—
> Strange faces, like to men in masquerade,

And here perhaps a monster, there a saint:
The spring gush'd through grim mouths of granite made,
And sparkled into basins, where it spent
Its little torrent in a thousand bubbles,
Like man's vain glory, and his vainer troubles. (XIII. 65. 1-8)

The mansion's self was vast and venerable,
With more of the monastic than has been
Elsewhere preserved: The cloisters still were stable, (XIII. 66. 1-3)

In such an eccentric place which has imaginative objects and fears, this marvelous profusion of the supernatural and the fantastic feelings situated beyond nature could give a magical sublime. Linked to the poetic and visionary power in the poem, the sublime also evokes excessive emotions. This kind of sublimity caused from sensual and erotic love is congenial to the gothic atmosphere. Byron's gothic arrangement here is to convey a possibility of unlimited love. According to Botting, "[g]othic texts were also seen to be subverting the mores and manners on which good social behavior rested" (4). In other words, there is a kind of power existing in such a frightening world in which the gothic figures could encounter more exciting adventurous freedom that transgressed the proper limits of social orders in the overflow of inner emotions.

Referring to the gothic elements in *Don Juan*, Byron

means to disclose women's individual power in their sexualities through the transgressive performance of gender reversal. Fitz-Fulke, who is interested in prank, dresses herself as a morbid ghost to seduce Juan as her victimized lover. Through the point of transvestism, the Duchess' disguised as a gothic villain can be seen as a woman who appropriates the male property and operates it as a sort of female power. In this perspective of masquerade, Terry Castle also mentions the belief of transvestism that "it encouraged female sexual freedom, and beyond that, female emancipation generally" ("Eros and Liberty" 164)[6]. Within the atmosphere of gothic terror, Fitz-Fulke's cross-dressing as the Black Friar not only signals the dismantling of male's prerogative sexual desire but also transcends women's inner fulfillment in their aspirations of love. The most important aspect is that Byron adopts the gothic technique to establish a revolutionary opportunity for shaping the conventional gender code of man/woman position.

Generally speaking, the gothic figures bear horrible features and threaten most humanist values, transgressing the common social standard and its stable authority. That is to say, such a defiant figure can be represented as a villain who rebels against the constraints of social mores. Similarly, Fitz-Fulke's disguised

6 This essay "Eros and Liberty at the English Masquerade, 1710-90," written by Terry Castle, is abbreviated as "Eros and Liberty" in this book.

as a ghost possesses a subversive energy of the gothic figure, fulfilling her personal desire to get emancipation from the social bonds: to get rid of the hypocritical restraint of being a docile lady and entangle Juan through frightening him into her arms. In such a gender reversal, Juan plays the role of being a virtuous heroine who is violated by the masculine threatening. In this light, the Black Friar pretended by Fitz-Fulke enables her to use the uncanny power to make Juan suffer the patriarchal tyranny. In fact, such an uncanny prank affirms the Duchess' feminine quality and female power to appropriate the male authority, sharpening her own individuality by means of an active pursuit of love.

Significantly, the gothic ambiences and the cross-dressing not only cause the uncanny gender reversal but also symbolize a kind of transcendence of inner emotion generated through the expulsion of exciting sensual stimulation. In Botting's point of view, "[t]error evoked cathartic emotions and facilitated the expulsion of the object of fear. Transgression, provoking fears of social disintegration, thus enabled the reconstitution of limits and boundaries" (7-8). For Juan, this is an unprecedented experience of gothic fear which fragments his personal masculine identity:

> Juan was petrified; he had heard a hint

Of such a spirit in these halls of old,
But thought like most men there was nothing in't
Beyond the rumour which such spots unfold, (XVI. 22. 1-4)

Once, twice, thrice passed, repassed the thing of air,
Or earth beneath or heaven or t'other place,
And Juan gazed upon it with a stare,
Yet could not speak or move; but on its base
As stands a statue, stood; He felt his hair
Twine like a knot of snakes around his face;
He taxed his tongue for words, which were not granted,
To ask the reverend person what he wanted. (XVI. 23. 1-8)

In this moment, Juan is frightened and powerless to face such a terrified figure. Haunted by such a dubious figure, Juan feels that "An age — expectant, powerless, with his eyes / Strain'd on the spot where first the figure gleam'd" (XVI. 25. 2-3), which produces an unknown confusion. When Juan at last advances to discover the truth of the gothic figure, he experiences a horrible excitement—an adventurous freedom on the path to love. As Byron describes:

Juan put forth one arm — Eternal powers!
It touched no soul nor body, but the wall, (XVI. 120. 1-2)

But still the Shade remained: the blue eyes glared,

And rather variably for stony death;
Yet one thing rather good the grave had spared,
The ghost had a remarkably sweet breath:
A straggling curl showed he had been fiarhaired,
A red lip, with two vows of pearls beneath, (XVI. 121. 1-6)

And Juan, puzzled, but still curious, thrust
His other arm forth — Wonder upon wonder!
It pressed upon a hard but glowing bust,
Which beat as if there was a warm heart under. (XVI. 122. 1-4)

The ghost, if ghost it were, seemed a sweet soul
As ever lurked beneath a holy hood:
A dimpled chin, a neck of ivory stole
Forth into something much like flesh and blood;
Back fell the sable frock and dreary cowl,
And they revealed — alas! that e'er they should!
In full, voluptuous, but not o'ergrown bulk,
The phantom of her frolic Grace — Fitz-Fulke! (XVI. 123. 1-8)

Byron's portrayal for both sexes as a reversal signals that Juan is a terrified heroine, and Fitz-Fulke is an aggressive love hunter. Implicit in the poem is that when Juan and Fitz-Fulke make their belated appearances at breakfast the next morning, they start having a skeptical love affair in a particularly alluring way.

Juan even looks as though he has fought with more than one supernatural spirit:

> Which best is to encounter — ghost or none,
> 　'Twere difficult to say — but Juan looked
> As if he had combated with more than one,
> 　Being wan and worn, with eyes that hardly brooked
> The light that through the Gothic windows shone:
> 　Her Grace too had a sort of air rebuked —
> Seemed pale and shivered, as if she had kept
> A vigil or dreamt rather more than slept. (XVII. 14. 1-8)

In this love making hint, Fitz-Fulke's cross-dressed male apparel really becomes a symbol of her inner drive and relief of sexuality. With male attire, Fitz-Fulke symbolically violates the fixed gender codes and establishes her individuality and privilege based on her decisive mind to pursue the ideal love. Though her temporal disguised as a ghost is disclosed at last, she experiences the sudden awe and sublimity accompanied by the lustful prank in her quest for love. Byron's technique of gothic elements brings out the feeling of sublime, which echoes what Botting says—"[g]othic produced emotional effects on its readers rather than developing a rational or properly cultivated response" (4). Obviously, Byron means to let us feel the passionate heart and the magnificent power of love under the carnival masquerade.

In short, Byron's digressive technique of gender reversal and gothic element are both used to show the transgressive power of female sexuality. As a passionate romanticist, Byron does not allow the ideal love itself to be corrupted. He tries so hard to build up the picture of a natural romantic love to its consummation with an unusual writing skill. Thus, we see Byron uses a lot of ironic tone to satirize the hypocritical society and despotic regulation. *Don Juan* really offers a medium for telling the truth of life with the romantic spirits—the emancipation from restrictions and conventions. In this poem, Byron depicts a world of female figures to celebrate his intention of sexual freedom. In other words, women are not only the so-called second sex or inferior civilization. Women have their own rights to choose their love and the ways they live. It is Byron's love of liberty and hatred of cant that make us think about women's problems of love or equality. Since we find Byron uses female sexuality as a sort of subversive power to grasp considerable freedom, *Don Juan* can be seen as a sort of revolutionary work to be against the old system and male-oriented thinking which the Lake poets stick to invariably. In this poem, Byron shows that women enjoy the pleasure in pursuit of love without repressing their sexual desires. Moreover, the freedom of female sexuality is worth considering in the modern era. In terms of equality and independence, only by freeing her sexuality can the measure of her individual's autonomy be reached. Byron's *Don Juan* indeed subverts the traditional concept of sexuality and offers a model for female's sexual freedom.

Spring Languages in the Spring Rain

Who and who disturbed the first warm and cold Spring?
Those misty drizzled gazes.
The eyes are delicately trapped, reading flowers'
hints.
Bloom shyly—the unexpected love story
after early Spring.

The look—is seen through the unusually beating mind.
Met who? Every rain has different interpretation.
Researched between the lines, each kind of bookbinding has different
realization.

The sound—is heard with a sympathetic response.
Spring languages in the spring rain congealed the wet eyes.
Eventually they could not tell who does the haze figure belong to.

But what the eyes said let every second of the time be back.
The red of peach blossom, after all, occupied the Spring
after words.

——*Cheng-Fen Chen*

Chapter Three

Female Identity

Introduction

In *Don Juan*, Juan's constant traveling and love encounters give him a feeling of loss and gain, like the pain and pleasure of love. We can further this feeling that Byron's embrace of exile and love is a strategy of conveying his liberal concept whereby departure multiplies possibilities. And Byron's combination of traveling and love is used to describe the irresistible attraction of love. Through a journey, a person can get rid of his usual inhibitions from surroundings and is forced to face various unpredictable things. Don Juan, an exiled foreigner, restrains himself from his mother's sexual education and tastes many different types of love. In other words, whenever Juan is seduced by women and ends up being a single man, he moves to other countries where he adventures more love seduction. Such new stimulation from new environments and amorous desires offers Juan a fresh impact, but meanwhile, a kind of treatment for his lost love. Byron's arrangement of Haidee's encounter with Juan, which makes him forget Julia, can be a good example here. Actually, the journey theme tells us one can get out of the old confinement and furthermore deal with more trivial problems in daily life. Additionally, one can face a lot of unpredictable things through traveling, like love, friendships, and thinking. In the poem, Juan encounters different types of women with whom he can broaden his horizons, letting new concepts and consciousness refresh his mind. Though we see digressions in the narrative, the centrality of Byron's *Don Juan* is the combination of freedom and love between two sexes. Thus, in these different love affairs in different countries, we find these female figures become more individualized through their pursuit of love. Put another way, not only men but also women can enjoy the erotic pleasure and refrain themselves from the orthodox confinement in the discourse of love.

In order to make the importance of female sexuality and female emancipation the central theme of *Don Juan*, and in order to direct increasing attention to them, Byron uses digressive technique and ironic tone to depict an ideal of equality between men and women. Important as are the digressions and the adventures of the hero to reinforce the narrative, Byron simultaneously presents emotional experiences and makes comments on his ideal freedom. Juan's adventure brings him new opportunities to love and new challenges of his own national identity. These female figures also have more chances to realize themselves through recognizing Juan within themselves. Though their love is filled with struggles and obstacles, these experiences firmly make them understand their inner voices and not to be subject to surrounding bonds. Especially for women, their dominance for Juan's love is a representation of women's independent individualities. Likewise, Juan's foreigner role is like a child, who lost his mother in each country, feels safe to be together with these passionate mother-like lovers. In my thinking, the women-Juan relationships in this poem represent a liberal trend for love. And the active performances of sexualities are self-realizations of women's erotic aspirations for their bodies or spirits.

Stranger, Speed and Space

As Juan's adventures move, the function of the digressions is more apparent and brings out kaleidoscopic backgrounds in which we see Byron's mobility and vitality of the whole work. In light of this, "*Don Juan* has not one style but a 'multiplicity of styles' or tones—what has been called the 'medley' style" (Trueblood, *Lord Byron* 153). Such an exotic traveling offers various incidents, ranging from romantic situations to realistic events. The narrativity involves ironic tone, burlesque, and serious comment, suggesting a free style of energy which is rebellious to the ancient Western literary styles. Alvin Kerman says that there is "a vital forceful onward movement" (qtd. in Paglia 355) in *Don Juan*, and "[s]peed is western domination of space, a linear track of the aggressive will" (Paglia 355). From the Spanish hometown to the Regency England in *Don*

Juan, Byron makes a change in the nature of space with forceful speed, which gives us an immediate impression on his mobility and his intended comprehension. Palgia mentions "*Don Juan* marks the first appearance in art of modern speed" (355), and the poem can be considered revolutionary from the perspective of its content or form. All these unstable writing techniques mentioned above in literary creativity signify Byron's passion and devotion to freedom. The theme between traveling and love is clear here: the hero's adventure lurks the great changes of love and erotics, as waves rise and recede in the sea. Regardless of the underlying risks, Juan and the female characters all seize the chance to love. No matter what kinds of risks await them, they cannot help falling into the world of love. As to the relation between women and love in *Don Juan*, Byron's liberty-based mind makes female's independence as for seeking happiness not a dream. That is to say, female sexuality becomes a powerful energy to support her actions while questing for love. Thus, the women-Juan relations need to be scrutinized carefully for the sake of seeing Byron's attitude toward women and love.

As we see the sexual implication is involved with the delineation of the quest for love, we find that the poetry portrays a distinctive eroticism of desire, the theme of 'carpe diem' and emancipation of women. Based upon the happiness and loving desire, Byron holds on to the principle of hedonism:

But the fact is that I have nothing planned,
Unless it were to be a moment merry—
A novel word in my vocabulary. (IV. 5. 6-8)

But coughs will come when sighs depart— and now
And then before sighs cease, for oft the one
Will bring the other, ere the lake-like brow
Is ruffled by a wrinkle, or the Sun
Of Life reached ten o'clock: and while a glow,
Hectic and brief as summer's day nigh done,
O'erspreads the cheek, which seems to pure for clay,
Thousands blaze, love, hope, die—how happy they!—
(X. 8. 1-8)

Byron senses the speed of age moves quickly in a transient form. According to Paglia, "[t]ransience, from the Latin transeo, contains the ideas both of travel and of the short live" (Paglia 358). Therefore, from the form and the traveling in *Don Juan*, Byron has readers pay attention to the limit of time as well as the ephemerality of love. The following is Byron's view of love and life:

All who have loved or love will still allow
Life has nought like it ... (VI. 6. 4-5)

Oh Love! Oh Glory! What are ye who fly

Around us ever, rarely to alight?
There's not a meteor in the polar sky
Of such transcendent and more fleeting flight. (VII. 1. 1-4)

They fell as thick as harvests beneath hail,
Grass before scythes, or corn below the sickle,
Proving that trite old truth that Life's as frail
As any other boon for which men stickle. (VIII. 43. 1-4)

No matter how much one obtains through life, one still faces the inevitable death. Fortune, reputation, and war are all a sort of things which Byron sees less important than love. Since human beings' lives are short, why not seize the time to chase the true love? Love cannot be measured in terms of money or be forced through tyranny. Byron here points out the fragility of life, so he admires the emotional love which could bring anything different in one's daily life.

Women–Juan Relationships: Chora and Abject

As I analyze the female characters, female sexualities, and their relations with Juan, I indeed sense a kind of subversive energy gradually emerging. During Juan's each traveling to different countries, the feeling of loss and the exotic experience of love are related to women. In conjunction with Byron's depiction of society as mobile shifting, Juan's potential loss refers to the gradual loss of dominance in love and in general or particular cultures. But the basic idea of the traveling is the "passionate love" or the loss of any innocent feeling. Such a romantic love is compared as: "In play, there are two pleasures for your choosing— / The one is winning, and the other losing" (XIV. 12. 7-8). In *Don Juan*, these women all choose to love even at expense of their own lives. And they play a dominant role in their affairs with Juan. At the same time, they also feel the struggles of love between Juan—they wants to come closer to him but are faced with some obstacles. Nonetheless, they choose to challenge the patriarchy and outside limits instead of losing the chance to love. These women's behaviors and emotions are all kinds of rebellious and independent spirits to the phallocentric society. The female consciousness is not subject to definite positions, rules, boundaries, or limits. And the maternal-like love is so strong but filled with struggles that the position of such love becomes abjected. But in terms of women's active quest for love, their love finally saves Juan's feeling of being empty and the impossibility of being settled down. It can be inferred that this kind of abject-like love becomes a subversive power to be against the male symbolic order. This is what Byron's admiration for women's decisive and active minds, and his metaphors of such exotic loving relations can also be the pathway to his basic philosophical thinking toward the balanced relation between both sexes.

Each journey is a door open to love; each female dominance of love is a representation of self-realization. Love is borderless, so are human beings' erotic desires. From the standpoints of these female figures depicted in the poem, Juan becomes a foreigner to them with whom they can recognize themselves. At the same time, they are attractive to Juan, wanting to unite with Juan to save his feeling of loss in an exotic country. And their love toward Juan is faced with outside social limits but full of challenging potentials. Thus, the women-Juan affairs actually can be seen as a mother-son relationship that Kristeva defines as "chora" in which women gradually reveal their subversive powers to counter patriarchal regulation. In this point of view, the females' aspirations of love in *Don Juan* can be considered rational. Even though women encounter obstacles in the pursuit of love, they still develop their own individual identities more and more.

In the definition of Kristeva's "chora," this is a place where an infant desires to contact his mother. Kristeva thinks Freud's and Lacan's concepts of the female are negative: they only see female as a male desire. Inherited from psychoanalytical thinking, she takes notes of the maternal body much more. The function of a mother is of having a phallic; the maternal quality becomes an ambiguous space. The mother is not a subject, but a part of the union with the infant. That is to say, the mother is a desirable Other, an unspeakable part in the infant's repressed mind. In Kristeva's *Strangers to Ourselves*, she mentions that there is a secret and unknown drive which leads the foreigner to wandering. In the exile, "if one has the strength not to give in, there remains a path to be discovered." (*Strangers* 5). In other words, all limits or difficulties are indifferent to him; meanwhile, in the unknown theory, "the foreigner is a stranger to his mother and asks nothing of her ... thus, has lost his mother" (*Strangers* 5). Relations to the other are just founded on relations to the other within oneself. Because of the continuous traveling, the foreigner challenges both the identity of the group and his own recognition in different places. When the stranger faces the loss of his mother, he also owns the possibility of owning the maternal relations with others. In such a borderless journey, "the subject can relate to an other because the other is within the subject" (Oliver 5). Krsiteva's idea in *Strangers to Ourselves* conveys an ambiguous relation in which the subject accepts the object in a moment but still may reject such connection between them. This two-way tension is correspondent with Kristeva's "abject" concept, which is something repulsive that both attracts and repels. Though painful and fascinating, the abject in such a mother-son relation can even threaten the patriarchal system, the symbolic order. This is what

Kristeva talks about in her "chora," which offers a deconstructing power to face the phallocentric thinking.

Kristeva suggests that the space of the mother-child bond is a semiotic "chora" which provides the maternal with the possibility to subvert the symbolic patriarchy. She further states that, "the mother-child relation as one marked by conflict: the child struggles to break free but the mother is reluctant to release it.... The maternal body becomes a site of conflicting desires" (qtd. in Creed 67). When the child attempts to break away with his mother, the mother becomes an 'abject' with which the child struggles to become a separate subject. However, "party consumed by the desire to remain locked in a blissful relationship with the mother and partly terrified of separation, the child finds it easy to succumb to the comforting pleasure of the dyadic relationship" (Creed 67). In other words, Kristeva's idea about the maternal figure is different from Freud's and Lacan's ideas of seeing women as a subordinate role to men. According to Kristeva, "with the subject's entry into the symbolic, which separates the child from the mother, the maternal figure and the authority she signifies are repressed" (Creed 69). Thus, when the child contacts the "chora" space, an unspeakable maternal/feminine power acts as an interruption to the symbolic order. Namely, the repressing maternal body represents a kind of subversion to the masculine order through the 'abjecting' process. Though the nature of the abjection both repels and attracts the subject and the object, the underlying energy of its potential emerges accordingly. Referring to the Law of the Father, Kristeva "regards the symbolic as the condition of ordered regulated, and rule-governed signification" (qtd. in Grosz 151). Then Kristeva's semiotic "chora" provides the order of the sexual drives to emanate and circulate, showing the 'feminine' compulsion to engulf the subject. From this point of view, the maternal function can be seen as phallic, and its subversive power transgresses the limits of the symbolic world.

Such an ambiguous space "chora" is Kristeva's main concept of a horribly subversive power. This feminine space makes a room for the role of mother who is negative and ignored in the symbolic order. Thus, the 'abject' condition in fact is a kind of recognition to the lack—the repressed feminine space:

> If it be true that the abject simultaneously beseeches and pulverizes the subject, one can understand that it is experienced at the peak of its strength when that subject … The abjection of self would be culminating form of that experience of the subject to which it is revealed that all its objects are based merely on the inaugural loss that laid the foundations of its own being. (*Powers of Horror* 5)

In other words, even though the infant enters into the Symbolic order through the abjection with his mother, he is still in the condition of feminine space where he gets the protection. And the feminine space will not disappear; instead, such feminine space is just oppressed in the unconsciousness and becoming a sort of subversive power in the patriarchal symbolic order.

From the point of Kristeva's "chora" and the "abjecting" process, the women-Juan relations just echo such theory of feminine space in which there is a potential for deconstructing patriarchy. As a psychoanalytic feminist, Kristeva furthers Freud's and Lacan's ideas toward love and oedipal relations. Actually, Kristeva thinks that the mother-son relation replaces the one between father and son. The maternal body's potential is evoked through the interaction with her child and love. In other words, through the contact with the child, she is no longer a subordinate role to the patriarchal one. Instead, the maternal figure becomes a desired object to the child, who is the subject in the repellent and seductive abjection. Kristeva also proposes that "the subject be understood as an 'open system'" (qtd. in Lechte 183). This means that rather than thinking of the outside world of the others as a threat, we should see it as a "stimulus to change and adaptation" (Lechte 183). In my opinion, Juan's adventurous exile is indeed correspondent to Kristeva's idea of seeing the subject as an 'open system.' Juan meets a variety of women with whom he not only goes through exotic love experiences but also has his personality become more mature than before. As for these female characters, they gradually enjoy the pleasure that love brings about and build their individual recognition through their active pursuit for their ideal love.

Though the painful and the attractive of this love-seeking experience both exist, erotic love and female sexuality accompanied by passionate hearts are the main irresistible instincts that Byron would like to emphasize and cherish. By means of the unknown adventure and difficulty, people will be increasingly more capable of love. Thus, the greater love is, the less obstacles one will encounter. Therefore, love and personal breakthrough are mutual openness of an individual's psyche. In *Don Juan*, the tension of love emerges from the seeming mother-son relation between the love-desired women and passive Juan. In his passivity, Juan actually falls into a series of romantic situations at each country: he attracts various dominant women—Julia, Haidee, the "imperious" Gulbeyaz, the "devouring" Catherine, the "full-blown" Fitz-Fulke, and Adeline, "The fair most fatal Juan ever met" (XIII. 12. 3). Their relations between Juan are just ambiguous because these potentially deadly women are like mother and lover at the same time. Nonetheless, Byron's intention is that women develop their own identities through such an ambiguous role—mother or lover. Under such a strong erotic power, Juan cannot resist the fusion of these females' love, just like an infant who cannot separate her mother's maternal love. From this depiction of maternal potential in the discourse of love, women are no longer just thought of as men's objects. Instead, they represent their natural feelings of amorous love and then subvert the previous chains for women, such as being housekeepers, chaste wives, or repressive mothers. Under Byron's ironic delineation of women, thus we find that women do not hide their emotions but behave their love instincts spontaneously. Even any uncertainty of this love exists, they still go to meet it. The young Juan, though a stranger to these women, offers chances for those women to own their rights to pursuit love and fulfill their feminine desires with sexuality performances.

With the changes that take place in time, the possibilities of feeling of loss and gain are easily happened to the foreigners and the outside strangers in a traveling. In the shifting world of *Don Juan*, the amorous atmosphere is filled with such sweet and painful feelings, which can be seen as a loving worth at expense of one's everything, even life. As for Juan, "[t]earing oneself away from family, language, and country in order to settle down elsewhere is a daring action accompanied by sexual frenzy: no more prohibition, everything is possible" (*Strangers* 30). Such a borderless opportunity brings about happiness to the foreigner Juan. Meanwhile, by recognizing him within themselves, these female figures disclose the hidden faces of their identities. From the constantly changing space, Juan is like an orphan who is consumed by his love for a lost mother. Love and sexuality become the women-Juan affairs, illustrating Byron's concern on erotics between two sexes based on his passionately liberal thinking. In the poem, Juan's existence indeed helps women show their passions and build self-independent values. What's more, in *Don Juan*, one's sexual passion is "the controlless core of human heart" (I. 116. 3-4), continually breaking through the orthodoxy patterns of social values as well as refusing to be stultified and reasserting its potentially turbulent power. Thus, from the fluid mobile rhetoric tones and digressive technique, female sexuality and its maternal function reveals the request for love and individuality. Here I examine Julia's improper love toward Juan, Haidee and Juan's innocent love, and the Russian Catherine's tyrannical love toward Juan in the following paragraphs. These women show their desired love for Juan in active ways; they also protect Juan as their son-like lover.

Julia's sexuality and passionate seduction of Juan makes him realize the taste of love. In order to depict Julia's dominant love, Byron places Juan in the place of his subordination to women. In other words, the more sophisticated Julia treats the son-like Juan as her destined lover in her terrible marriage: "Juan she saw and as a pretty child / Caressed him often ..." (I.

69. 1-2). This mother-son pattern emphasizes not only Juan's weakness to be against love but also Julia's maternal dominance over this love encounter. From the beginning to the end, Julia experiences fulfillment and temptation in her interaction with Juan. Behind the passionate heart is also the struggling toward her religion or society. Nonetheless, the stronger erotic love triumphs every outside limits even if she is immured in a convent. In this canto, Byron carefully delineates Julia's changes in her mood:

> But passion most dissembles yet betrays
>   Even by its darkness; as the blackest sky
> Foretells the heaviest tempest, it displays
>   Its working through the vainly guarded eye,
> And in whatever aspect it arrays
>   Itself, 't is still the same hypocrisy;
> Coldness or Anger, even Disdain or Hate
> Are masks it often wears, and still too late. (I. 73. 1-8)

> Then there were sighs, the deeper for suppression,
>   And stolen glances, sweeter for the theft,
> And burning blushes, though for no transgression,
>   Tremblings when met, and restlessness when left;
> All these are little preludes to possession,
>   Of which young passion cannot be bereft,

> And merely tend to show how greatly love is
> Embarrass'd at first starting with a novice. (I. 74. 1-8)

> She now determined that a virtuous woman
> Should rather face and overcome temptation,
> That flight was base and dastardly … (I. 77. 1-3)

Julia's decisive mind is clearly seen here, that is, to face any danger or threatening in this love. Faced with her erotic desire, Julia feels empowered and pursues Juan actively. On the contrary, Juan's hiding under the bed and remaining passive in Julia's seduction shows that he is still the pawn of an older woman. Regardless of his precocious-prevention education, he accepts Julia's hearty kisses. In terms of "chora" and "abject," both Julia and Juan break the patriarchal system as primacy. Instead, their mutual love represents a kind of femininity recognition gradually emerges. In other words, the lover experiences a kind of sublimity in their struggling-filled love, which not only dismantles the symbolic realm but also builds a feminine power harmonized by Julia and Juan's mother-son relation. Meanwhile, the magnetism of love also changes one's mind and outside appearance:

> How beautiful she looked! Her conscious heart
> Glowed in her cheek, and get she felt no wrong:
> Oh Love, how perfect is thy mystic art,

Strengthening the weak and trampling on the strong!
How self-deceitful is the sagest part
Of mortals whom thy lure hath led along! —
The precipice she stood on was immense,
So was her creed in her own innocence. (I. 106. 1-8)

Here Byron points out female sexuality becomes confident and assertive through love's magic. We can see Julia's bravery and decision strengthen her own erotic desire. Therefore, the importance of love is also elevated in that it is a powerful drive underlying in every human beings' hearts. Like men, women are empowered to follow their own minds, fulfilling their love desires actively and decisively. *Don Juan* thus conveys such a crucial sentimental emotion to emphasize the liberal concept toward both men and women optimistically.

The most cherished female sexuality not only lies in Julia's active pursuit of love but also lies in her consciousness of those difficult circumstances that hinder her love. Also, Julia wants to know herself and at last knows herself more and more:

'I loved, I love you, for that love have lost
State, station, Heaven, Mankind's, my own esteem,
And yet cannot regret what it hath cost,
So dear is still the memory of that dream;
Yet if I name my guilt, 'tis not to boast,

None can deem harshlier of me than I deem:
I trace this scrawl because I cannot rest —
I've nothing to reproach or to request. (I. 193. 1-8)

This is a female figure of knowing the consequence of sinfulness but being stick to her own faith: born to love. This strong faith is even at expense of everything in her life. Though painful, Julia's erotics toward Juan becomes a kind of redemption in her unhappy marriage. Faced with such a handsome young Juan, Julia excludes any limits and go to embrace Juan's threatening attraction. Like a mother who wants to protect her child, Julia's union with Juan breaks the patriarchal law of strengthening masculine dominance. This is because love and passion occupy her whole mind:

'You will proceed in beauty and in pride,
Beloved and loving many. All is o'er
For me on earth, except some years to hide
My shame and sorrow deep in my heart's core:
These I could bear, but cannot cast aside
The passion which still rends it as before,—(I. 195. 1-6)

My heart is feminine, nor can forget—
To all, except one image, madly blind;
So shakes the needle, and so stands the pole,

As vibrates my fond heart to my fix'd soul. (I. 196. 5-8)

Here the decisive femininity is fully evealed, and it also represents Byron's psyche to create such a female figure. Julia regards Juan as her "soul," her long-repressed desire. The description of Julia's inner self is also with a discourse placing desire at her own center. No matter how painful this love is, she cannot resist falling in love with Juan: "To love too much has been the only art / I used" (I. 192. 5-6). Additionally, she also speaks out the revelation of her poetic creator Byron whose structure of creation conveys his various sentimental thinking. In this episode, Byron arranges Julia meets Juan in love because love really can be a variety of forms. Byron depicts Julia's misery of her marriage, evoking out the pressing concern to such difficulty a woman suffers. This "feminine heart" indeed becomes a pathway to Byron's liberal thinking of erotics between men and women. And through this feminine heart, the importance of love and women's individualities are also strengthened. From this, it can be seen that Julia's love toward Juan is her feminine dominance to protect her lover and defend her inner spiritual mind.

With Juan's next adventure to the Greek island, we see Byron's another view of love, which is more passionate and purer as people's natural feelings. As to Julia's love toward

Juan, this is an eternal feeling that exists in her mind. Actually, Byron's arrangement of Juan's next journey points out the unlimited possibility of love and the freedom of accepting love. Similarly, the exotic women all have the same chance to get along with this foreigner, even unfolding their sexual repression to build self-recognition. After all, liberal thinking and standard evoke free choices of love. In this point, Byron constructs a narrator more transgressive than himself. At the end of canto two, the narrator points out an unstable loving possibility and how love is suddenly evoked, which is a way of presenting the free concept toward human beings' emotions:

> I hate inconstancy — I loathe, detest,
>   Abhor, condemn, abjure the mortal made
> Of such quicksilver clay that in his breast
>   No permanent foundations can be laid;
> Love, constant love, has been my constant guest,
>   And yet last night, being at a masquerade,
> I saw the prettiest creature, fresh from Milan,
> Which gave me some sensations like a villain. (II. 209. 1-8)
>
> But soon Philosophy came to my aid,
>   And whispered, "Think of every sacred tie!"
> "I will, my dear Philosophy!" I said,
>   "But then her teeth, and then, Oh Heaven! her eye!

I'll just inquire if she be wife or maid,
    Or neither — out of curiosity."
"Stop!" cried Philosophy, with air so Grecian,
(Though she was masqued then as a fair Venetian;) (II. 210. 1-8)

The narrator reveals a strong power of love, which can change a person suddenly and is worth one's attention. In the Haidee episode, Byron portrays such a wonderful love happens in a paradise-like Eden. And the most important vision of Haidee-Juan's love is a totally selfless and fulfilling love relationship.

Haidee and Juan both appear as pure children who enjoy the delight of love in a bewildering adult world, but within the story their roles are distinguished clearly as follows: Haidee functions as a mother, and Juan becomes an infantile who needs maternal protection. As a stranger from Spanish, Juan suffers from shipwreck and terrible cannibal experience to the Greek island. When he drifts to the Greek island, he seems to be a child hurt by former experiences and is eager to have a warm hug. As Manning says, "[f]amished and half-drowned, Juan is reborn from the sea and nursed back to health in Haidee's warm, well-provisioned, and womb-like cave" ("Byron's Imperceptiveness" 112)[1]. Byron also uses tender words to describe their mother-son

---

1 This essay "*Don Juan* and Byron's Imperceptiveness to the English Word," written by Peter J. Manning, is abbreviated as "Byron's Imperceptiveness" in this book.

relations and intimate mutual attraction:

> And she bent o'er him, and he lay beneath,
>
> Hushed as the babe upon its mother's breast, (II. 148. 1-2)

> He ate, and he was well supplied: and she,
>
> Who watch'd him like a mother, would have fed
>
> Him past all bounds, because she smiled to see
>
> Such appetite in one she had deem'd dead:
>
> But Zoe, being older than Haidee,
>
> Knew (by tradition, for she ne'er had read)
>
> That famish'd people must be slowly nurst,
>
> And fed by spoonfuls, else they always burst. (II. 158. 1-8)

These similes and the narrative skill make Haidee and Juan, who have their own different races and languages, enter into the symbolized "union of mother and infant, at the early stage of human development before the infant comes to see himself as separate from the mother" ("Byron's Imperceptiveness" 112). Here Byron's delineation of Juan and Haidee's private love is a mutual attraction, like the dyad of mother and infant, both of whom count on each other to a world of completely reciprocal love.

Haidee's maternal love for Juan is involved with true appreciation and threatening amorous attraction. When Haidee first looks at Juan, she gradually develops her maternal instinct to protect Juan from outside danger or her father's aggression. As Lambro is ready to shoot Juan, Haidee "threw herself her boy before; / Stern as her sire: "On me," she cried, "let Death / Descend — the fault is mine ..." (IV. 42. 3-5). Such a great protection is parallel to the sacrifice of one's life, and all Haidee does is to save her only true love in her eternal life. Haidee's every minute and breath exist for her forever lover. Even though Haidee and Juan come from different countries, they go across the limits of continent border and love each other in a paradisal place. Besides, Haidee's maternity is influenced by her own mother, as Byron portrays as follows:

> The Moorish blood partakes the planet's hour,
> And like the soil beneath it will being forth:
> Beauty and love were Haidee's mother's dower;
> But her large dark eye showed deep Passion force,
> Though sleeping like a lion near a source. (IV. 56. 4-8)
>
> Her daughter, tempered with a milder ray,
> Like summer clouds all silvery, smooth, and fair,
> Till slowly charged with thunder they display
> Terror to earth, and tempest to the air,
> Had held till now her soft and milky way;
> But overwrought with passion and Despair,
> The fire burst forth from her Numidian veins,

Even as the simoom sweeps the blasted plains. (IV. 57. 1-8)

Byron uses the symbol of sun to describe Haidee's natural passion and decisive mind to win her love. The sun is not only the most striking thing to be seen but also the extreme condition of light. While seeing the sun's rays, Juan cannot resist such a strong direction of his lost mother. When Juan and Haidee unite together, Juan enjoys a great love in which the maternal concern of caring a baby is pervasive. Even Haidee's most maternally protective gestures imply a kind of nurturing power:

> And then she stopped and stood as if in awe
> (For sleep is awful), and on tiptoe crept
> And wrapt him closer, lest the air, too raw,
> Should reach his blood, then o'er him still as Death
> Bent, with hushed lips, that drank his scarce-drawn breath.
> (II. 143. 4-8)

These aspects of careful protection are also reinforced by their lack of communal language. Thus, the instances of wordlessness between Haidee and Juan are thematically connected to their seeming mother-son love relationship:

> Now Juan could not understand a word,
> Being no Grecian; but he had an ear,
> And her voice was the warble of a bird,

So soft, so sweet, so delicately clear,
That finer, simpler music ne'er was heard;
The sort of sound we echo with a tear,
Without knowing why, an overpowering tone,
Whence melody descends as from a throne. (II. 151. 1-8)

According to Manning's analysis, "[t]his characterization of Haidee's voice presents a familiar Romantic figure, at once pathetic and sublime. Voice is here an absolute presence, capable of doing without the agency of words and directing inspiring a response from its hearers" ("Byron's Imperceptiveness" 111). Byron displays multiple situations of love itself: when love exists between two people, their languages, voices, and eye contacts are various forms for conveying love. Furthermore, Haidee and Juan's love overcomes their natural differences in themselves. A lover's voice can also involve a powerful strength for protecting one's fragile heart or spirit. Haidee's voice just gives the stranger-like Juan a formless but tender feeling of security. The less Haidee and Juan can talk, the more intense loving atmosphere they can share:

And then fair Haidee tried her tongue at speaking,
But not a word could Juan comprehend,
Although he listened so that the young Greek in
Her earnestness would ne'er have made an end; (II. 161. 1-4)

And then she had recourse to nods and signs,
    And smiles and sparkles of the speaking eye,
And read (the only book she could) the lines
    Of his fair face and found, by sympathy,
The answer eloquent, where the soul shines
    And darts in one quick glance a long reply;
And turns in every look she saw exprest
A world of words, and things at which she guessed. (II. 162. 1-8)

And now by dint of fingers and of eyes,
    And words repeated after her, he took
A lesson in her tongue, but by surmise,
    No doubt less of her language than her look:
As he won studies fervently the skies
    Turns oftener to the stars than to his book,
Thus Juan learned his alpha *beta* better
From Haidee's glance than any graven letter. (II. 163. 1-8)

Therefore, their different races and freely usage of language become the very mark of their intimacy of mutual love. On the other hand, Haidee's teaching Greece for Juan is like a mother's careful teaching for her new born baby. As for Juan, he begins to learn new words and repeat the sounds with the foreign woman. And such feelings are "universal as the sun" (II. 167. 3). Here Byron develops the theme of their abilities to communicate without the mediation of words: "They felt no terrors from the night; they were / All in all to each other: though their speech / Was broken words, they thought a language there" (II. 189. 2-4). Even if there is love between Haidee and Juan, language is not necessary to them. Because of their mutual attraction, their hearts are also known with each other. What Haidee gives to Juan is her true passion, which is beyond the general fantasy of male's vision. A father can give a child a powerful identification; however, a mother's love can be compared as an ocean, in which her loving and pathetic care for a child is great and selfless. Thus, through Juan and Haidee's interaction, they both recognize themselves and depend on each other intimately.

In Haidee's canto, we can see women's humble hope for some acknowledgement and good treatment from men does not exist. Instead, we see her brave and sacrificing spirit to maintain her love. Actually, true love needs courage and temptation. Not only do Haidee and Juan enjoy the pleasure of love, but they also suffer from Lambro's interruption. So Haidee and Juan's situation is just like kristevian "chora" in which the mother and the child desire to be united but feel a kind of counter power against their communal harmony. Their sweet harmony of love faces challenges as Lambro returns:

> And Haidee clung around him, "Juan,' t is—

’Tis Lambro— ’tis my father! Kneel with me—
He will forgive us— yes— it must be— yes.
Oh dearest father, in this agony
Of pleasure and of pain, even while I kiss
Thy garment’s hem with transport, can it be
That doubt should mingle with my filial joy?
Deal with me as thou wilt, but spare this boy.” (IV. 38. 1-8)

Haidee’s words point out her inner voice of pursuing her unique lover: love is involved with pain and pleasure, like the ‘dark’ and ‘light’ aspects of things. Thus, they both suffer from the abjection of self, that is to say, their abjection is in fact not only a kind of recognition of the mutual want but also a suffering condition of outside terror. As Elizabeth Gross states that “[t]he abject defines a pre-oedipal space and self-conception: it is the space between subject and object, both repulsive and attractive, which threatens to draw the subject and its objects towards it, a space of simultaneous pleasure and danger” (94). Nonetheless, femininity and female sexuality in the “chora” space are not yet defined in the relation to the phallocentric order. Thus, the mother is like a phallic woman who does not desire to be regulated by masculinity but would like to protect her child with her feminine power. Haidee’s love toward Juan involves such a great maternal care, revealing her sexuality opposed to her patriarchal father. This is a woman's potential feminine power to defend her innocent love and self-subjectivity.

Love can bring hopes and changes for them, and its wonder even gives them a new thinking and different inspirations toward life values. In order to depict the wonder of love, Byron creates an ideal paradise filled with romantic ambiences in which his imagination works. In such a romantic atmosphere, the amorous elements incite the atmosphere of sublime. Kristeva also talks about the sublime in her *Powers of Horror*: "In the symptom, the abject permeates me, I became abject. Through sublimation, I keep it under control. The abject is edged with the sublime" (11). In Haidee-Juan affair, their love permeates each other in the abject-struggled love relationship. Nonetheless, their love conquers obstacles between them and represents a brave spirit of pursuing what they want. Not only does love create sublimity between them, but it also keeps any hampering difficulty under control. In the poem, we can easily sense the awful, tender, and natural harmony between Juan and Haidee:

> It was a wild and breaker-beaten coast,
>   With cliffs above an d a broad sandy shore,
> Guarded by shoals and rocks as by an host,
>   With here and there a creek, whose aspect wore
> A better welcome to the tempest-toast;

And rarely ceased the haughty billow's roar,
Save on the dead long summer days, which make
The outstretched Ocean glitter like a lake. (II. 177. 1-8)

They looked up to the sky, whose floating glow
Spread like a rosy Ocean, vast and bright;
They gazed upon the glittering sea below,
Whence the broad Moon rose circling into sight;
They heard the wave's splash and the wind so low,
And saw each other's dark eyes darting light
Into each other — and, beholding this,
Their lips drew near, and clung into a kiss; (II. 185. 1-8)

Amid such comfortable and pictorial scenery, their sexual passions are provoked deeply. Juan and Haidee can receive mutual love at the same time. Even though they don't have common language and belong to different races, they love freely because they have passions and young hearts. Haidee really realizes her precious love and also confronts her father to save her lover at expense of her own life.

As Byron ends Haidee and Juan's love as a tragedy, he conveys his central idea toward human beings: seize the time to love and enjoy anything it brings about. While facing Lambro's violence, Juan is protected as he is nursed by Haidee, like going back to accept a mother's warm hug. Byron uses a tragic setting to prove their pure love and Haidee's unregretful given to Juan. As Juan leaves Greek Island, he begins another trip constantly. At the same time, Byron still uses digression to intensify the strong love unified by Juan and his pursuers, like the fusion of infant and mother. From the paradisal Greek to the mysterious seraglio, Juan experiences love not regulated by social standard but evoked by natural desire of love. This time, Byron again digresses the main idea of pursuing love by means of the war episode. In the canto of Russia-Turkey war, Byron implicitly strengthens the importance of love through Catherine and Juan's interaction. Byron begins the description of Catherine the Great by expanding upon her aspiration of war to that of sexual passion:

> Oh Catherine! (for of all interjections,
>
> To thee both oh! And ah! belong, of right,
>
> In love and war.) How odd are the connections
>
> Of human thoughts, which jostle in their flight!
>
> Just now yours were cut out in different sections:
>
> First Ismail's capture caught your fancy quite;
>
> Next of new knights, the fresh and glorious hatch;
>
> And thirdly, he who brought you the dispatch. (IX. 65. 1-8)

Since Catherine sees Juan, her heart is no longer silent and gradually falls into the world of love. Even as a powerful queen, she undoubtedly opens her mind to the young Juan. However, Catherine is "Then recollecting the whole Empress, nor / Forgetting quite the woman ..." (IX. 58. 1-2). In this point, Catherine also suffers from a struggle between attraction and rebellion, which is like Kristevian "chora" generated from the fusion of mother and infant. That is, though Catherine feels herself as a woman with a noble status, she still loses her mind to the young messenger. Thus, we know Byron's intention here is to emphasize how important and indispensable love is to a woman. Love becomes the origin of human beings, and its power even decides life and death:

> Oh, thou *teterrima causa* of all "belli"—
>   Thou gate of life and death— thou nondescript!
> Whence is our exit and our entrance,— Well I
>   May pause in pondering how all souls are dipt
> In thy perennial fountain— how man fell I
>   Know not, since knowledge saw her branches stript
> Of her first fruit; but how he falls and rises
> Since, thou hast settled beyond all surmises. (IX. 55. 1-8)
>
> Some call thee 'the worst cause of war', but I
>   Maintain thou art the best: for after all
> From thee we come, to thee we go, and why

To get at thee not batter down a wall
Or waste a world? since no one can deny
Thou dost replenish worlds both great and small?
With — or without thee — all things at a stand
Are, or would be, thou Sea of Life's dry land! (IX. 56. 1-8)

Catherine, who was the grand Epitome
Of that great cause of War, or Peace, or what
You please (it causes all the things which be,
So you may take your choice of this or that) —
Catherine, I say, was very glad to see
The handsome herald, on whose plumage sat
Victory; and pausing as she saw him kneel
With his dispatch, forgot to break to break the seal. (IX. 57. 1-8)

What is implied here is not so much the victory of war, although there is a hint of that too, as the blindness of love which brings great change in Catherine's life. The lustful Catherine, behaving her aggression and sexual passion, is a woman of the terrifying image and engulfing force that must be resisted by Juan. Nonetheless, love still happens between them and becomes a kind of irresistible power which harmonizes their hearts:

Her Majesty looked down, the youth looked up —
And so they fell in love; — She with his face,

His grace, his God-knows-what: for Cupid's cup
    With the first draught intoxicates apace,
A quintessential laudanum or "Black Drop,"
    Which makes one drunk at once, without the base
Expedient of full bumpers; for the eye
In love drinks all life's fountains (save tears) dry. (IX. 67. 1-8)

Obviously, Byron admires appreciation between lovers because love is a natural feeling which is hard to explain but happens suddenly. Here, the 'eye' image represents the catalyst of their love because eyes can express thought and feeling. According to Ferber's definition of eye, eye is "[t]he most prominent and expressive of facial features as well as the organs of sight" (70). When Catherine has eye contact with Juan, she is totally fascinated by Juan's eyes that are full of joy and grace. Thus, love just inflames at this moment and cannot be controlled with reason.

As we see Byron's portrayal of Catherine the Great, we understand that the pleasure of her love is natural and an active pursuing experience if it is not interfered by social conventions. Indeed, there is no hierarchy between Catherine and Juan's love. Instead, Catherine's sexuality is released greatly to win her ideal lover, like her troops destroying Ismail to win the victory. The narrator also says that Juan falls into "self-love," (IX. 68. 3) which is related to Kristeva's thinking that the desire for uniting with mother is close to the child's love of self. According to Kristeva, "[t]he child becomes the abject in order to avoid both separation from, and identification with, the maternal body—both equally painful, both equally impossible" (qtd. in Oliver 60). In other words, the child cannot resist the maternal body just because he cannot be free of it. And the maternal body is like a devouring body that evokes rage and fear. Thus, under Catherine's feminine power, Juan "sighed for beauty" (X. 37. 8) and falls into the world of Catherine's mother-like love. In the Catherine stanzas, Byron portrays the female amorous desire as a liberation which both Juan and Catherine obtain as a result of their mutual attraction.

Becoming Catherine's male mistress, Juan embraces her maternal-like protection and active passion. In other words, Juan's passivity in love relation and the disruption of building his patriarchal image are caused by this potentially deadly woman, a figure full of amorous desire and feminine subjectivity. For Catherine, she builds her individuality through the young foreigner; for Juan, he tastes the limitless opportunity of love in his journey. And the moral standard that Juan's mother sticks to does exist anymore. Instead, Donna Inez here praises Catherine's "maternal love" (X. 32. 8) and also acknowledges that Juan has a brother born with a step father. What Byron implies here is that the convention of moral behavior can be broken, and women have the same right to choose their happiness and experience this passionate love.

The Recognition of Female Identity

Generally speaking, Byron's female characters in *Don Juan* are of decisive and active passions toward their love. In traditional patriarchal society, women are almost seen as the function of being mothers without self identity or subjectivity. But in Byron's liberal mind, he uses shifting ways of narrative tone and digression to depict women's another side: they are full of potentials to resist the orthodoxy of regulation. Although they face the struggle whether they should choose Juan as lover or not, they try this experience of love and make themselves more independent in this abject process. Kristeva ever says that the abject is "what disturbs identity, system, order" (*Powers of Horror* 4). Within the abjection with Juan, these women already subvert the patriarchal law of making women as a subordinate role. Similarly, to the child, the abject appears as the struggle to separate from the mother. Thus, whenever Juan meets the foreign women, he feels a kind of raging attraction but cannot resist the maternal power. For Juan, these female bodies become the object of love. And love between Juan and women is generated from both their passionate and amorous instincts. Meanwhile, their eoncounters generate flexible self-realization for their susceptible individulities. For instance, Haidee's pusuit for the unlawful love is connected with Byron's freely erotic mind. Her natural expectation for freedom and love is recoded as revolutionary, which overturns the traditional assumptions about women. According to Donelan, "[t]his figure of the rebel daughter, freed from the constraints of patriarhy, is in the Haidee story conflated with the figure of the natural, nurturing mother of the Republic" (80). Beneath the Haidee episode is a exposure of the contradictions society that runs on the basis of conventional fantasy. For Byron, true freedom is based on the reality in life rather than the excesses of the public fantasy. Byron's digressive form of love stories in *Don Juan* is also a reflection of how women perceive their self-consciousness in the psycosocial mobility with Juan's love. And we see Byron's view of the importance of female sexuality and female emancipation in love.

Haidee, depicted as a figure of Liberty, performs her female sexuality bravely despite Lambro's disturbance of her love. Her protection of Juan is like a maternal concern; though she dies at last, she gets her eternally cherished love. In terms of Storey's idea, "an image of death and mourning becomes one of living passion, the volcano that in its eruption proves itself true" (207). That is to say, passion works out Haidee's direction of love. If love is reciprocal between Juan and Haidee, so too is the loss. And Haidee's death is also an indication of her warm heart, of her passion: "... her days and pleasures were / Brief, but delightful—such as had not staid / Long with her destiny…" (IV. 71. 5-7). Therefore, we know that one's sexual passion cannot be controlled by outside regulations because it is the natural core of one's heart. As to Inez's education for Juan's concept toward love, this is also what Byron cannot accept. The lack of loving affection jeopardizes every great possibility of unforgettable love. Byron thus satirizes sexual hypocrisy: "That Inez had, ere Don Alfonso's marriage / Forgot with him her very prudent carriage" (I. 66. 7-8). According to Manning, "[i]t is inevitable that Juan should seek to establish his autonomy, and Inez's desire to manage him by suppressing his sexuality pits against a force to which she herself is prey" ("The Byronic Hero" 47). Such a strong face comes from human beings' natural feelings—quest for the freedom of love. Since men can build their autonomy, women are also able to choose what they want. Though under the struggle between love and society value, Inez and Julia still break through the primary patriarchal patterns of consciousness and show their emotional powers bravely. This is women's refusal to be stultified only as a second role in both gender systems; however, they recognize themselves through sexual encounters more and more.

Everyone has the ability of pursuing love only if he or she regards the basic standard of freedom. In order to speak out women's sexuality in a positive way, Byron uses satire to describe women's various behaviors and appearances. No matter how difficult or struggling the tension of love is, women perform bravely to win Juan's heart. And the digressive settings all help to illustrate Byron's focus on the erotic love and liberal thinking toward both genders. For example, Byron uses war as a revolutionary movement to be against the established forms which regulated human beings' liberty. Wars are terrible, but they are justifiable in support of freedom. However, compared with love, war should be divested of its charm, Byron thought, in terms of its history. This is why we see Catherine the great, a noble queen of Russian, is subject to Juan's attractiveness more than the triumph of military conquest:

> History can only take things in the gross;
>   But could we know them in detail, perchance
> In balancing the profit and the loss,
>   War's merit it by no means might enhance,
> To waste so much gold for a little dross,
>   As hath been done, mere conquest to advance. (VIII. 3. 1-6)

> If here and there some transient trait of pity

Was shown, and some more noble heart broke through
Its bloody bond, and saved, perhaps some pretty
Child or an aged, helpless man or two —
What's this in one annihilated city,
Where thousand loves, and ties, and duties grow?
Cockneys of London! Muscadins of Paris!
Just ponder what a pious pastime War is. (VIII. 124. 1-8)

From this standpoint, war is merciless and does not give the individual the kind of honor and glory he is seeking. Byron uses the theme of war to emphasize the wonder of love. And war just becomes an idea for Byron to depict that people may obtain freedom at expense of their lives and peaceful minds. At this moment, love can change everything to warm human beings' hearts: "Love—that great opener of the heart and all / The ways that lead there, be they near or far, / Above, below, by turnpikes great or small" (IX. 80. 2-4). Catherine's active seduction of love makes her hearts tender and does anything for Juan. This is what Byron want to mention: just seize the chance to love and cherish the sublimity love brings about. All in all, with Kristeva's "chora" concept, these female figures suffer both from the internal consciousness and external society values. And their experiences of love are a destroyer and a preserver; each function may be either tears of joy or tears of pain. In this journey of love, all these women and Juan can do is to go ahead without hesitation.

Besides the importance of love, Byron furthermore mentions the theme of "carpe diem" in the poem: "This hourly dread of all! whose threaten'd sting / Turns life to terror, even though in its sheath: / Mark how its lipless mouth grins without breath" (IX. 11. 6-8). Hence for delineating his suggestion of seizing chances to love, Byron ceaselessly creates romantic love or forbidden love which his Juan encounters. In these various love affairs, Byron makes Juan get together with different types of women. On the surface, these women all tend to perform actively in quest of love. Underlying the female depiction is Byron's free will and rebellious spirit on women's satisfaction from love. Byron's concern here is also to illustrate the positive aspect of females' active pursuit of love and pleasure which they obtain through the process of seeking love. For love that dominates Byron's imagination of the world is not a ruling power or a social force. Instead, love is simply the source of life and energies. Based on liberal thinking, men or women bear the drive to enjoy love and seek their happiness. Byron's *Don Juan* indeed represents a kind of revolutionary idea toward both gender codes and its contents revise some traditional values on women.

Though suffering from pain and pleasure in the sea of

love, women show their sentimental passions and individual subjectivities based on the erotic feelings. According to Lorde, "[t]he erotic is a measure between the beginning of our sense of self and the chaos of our strongest feelings. It is an internal sense of satisfaction to which, once we have experienced it, we know we can aspire" (54). Women have their own intuitions and thoughts in love. Byron here points out women's natural feelings and their exaltation of love are worth praising and concerning more. And love is so wonderful that human beings should seize the time to fulfill the erotic in their endeavors and attempt to create a fair treatment for both sexes.

Each Star Has Its Name

The stars are no longer far away.
I found you, also knowing
your destiny.

Poisonous scorpion climbs up high, extracting
one golden ring in the wandering.
It does good things secretly.
Any moment is like fireworks.

But the black-dyed dream is already
occupied by the smallest star, which

does not let me be absent.

—— *Cheng-Fen Chen*

Chapter Four

Conclusion

From the Spanish Don Juan legend to Byron's adaptation of *Don Juan*, the most obvious transormations of the story are the women-Juan relationships. Put it differently, women are like love hunters whereas Juan is their love-questing victim. For me, under the surface of their affairs are their hearts of dreaming freedom in the sea of love. In the long run, women are repressed for their external behaviors and sexual desires. Actually, women's positions have been gradually elevated since Shakespeare's times but are not valued much. As the time comes to the Romantic period, the value of women is still developed into that they are subordinate to men. However, Byron's passionately romantic heart keeps women as the same level as men, which is different from other romantic poets. Based on his philosophically liberal thinking, everything should not be restrained but has many possibilities. Likewise, the loving relation opens to everyone without any limits, such as race, nation, and age. Thus, Byron uses different settings and exotic encounters to depict the limitless opportunity of love. The most important concept is that women own their right in their searching for love. In other words, love in *Don Juan* is so crucial to women that they are presented as the predators throughout. Implicit in this female's active sexuality is to build her more decisive and independent thinking. Byron, an advocator of liberty and love, depicts women in *Don Juan* by means of satire. However, he praises women's erotics, endeavoring to emancipate their oppressed minds from the constricting societies and social values. In this case, Byron envisions gender equality in this poem. Also, he shows great concern and sympathy to those miserable women who suffer from traditional constraints and unhappy marriage. For me, I really agree with Byron's thinking in his endeavor to strive for freedom. Only by being free to face anything can we cherish our autonomy and even strengthen our self-recognition.

Due to his mother's serious education and his liberating mind, Byron does not bear many chauvinistic attitudes toward women. In reality, some of his love experiences are started and directed by females. Byron at last does not waste his time since he knows that time and life are ephemeral and worth cherishing, albeit with regrets and pain in some of the memories of love. Thus, it is predicable that not just men can chase their lovely females, but women are also able to show their passions for seeking love with courage. Even Byron creates his ideal Haidee, a pure girl keeping her first love bravely, to express that the unorthodox female sexuality is on the rise. In other words, females' active pursuit of love is not supposed to be seen as irrational. Conversely, women's aspirations of love and care should also be respected. In this light, Byron is not a misogynist, though he was hurt by some of his lovers. Since men can have marriage or affairs with women, why can't women own their emotional independence? In terms of Byron's love of freedom and hatred of cant, he must make a voice for women and pinpoint the downside of excessive tyrannical female qualities. Meanwhile, he admires women's active seeking for love and the release of their sexualities—not merely the biological sex, but also the emotional satisfaction accompanied by their love experiences. This is why Byron portrays female figures as predators and Juan as a victim in the poem. Byron's intention not only depicts female's beauty like other romantic poets but also discloses women's oppressed situations and their gradual subversion of such traditional bonds through his use of satire. To put it simply, under Byron's cynical tone lies the true words for proper views about women. *Don Juan* is indeed such a revolutionary work that changes the conventional thinking about women in the discourse of love.

In *Don Juan*, Byron combines the neo-classical poetic style and the characteristics of romanticism. His adoption of Augustanism, the ironic manner, is influenced by Pope and used to depict women in anti-romantic forms. However, Byron stills makes the poem romantic in order to convey the wonderful paradise of love. Viewed in this way, *Don Juan* has a flexible form and style because of Byron's capricious personality and the transition from what is serious to what is burlesque. What's over, Byron's mobility is obviously shown through his theme of journey since *Childe Harold's Pilgrimage*. In this time, *Don Juan*'s mobile-written style and digression also reflect the traveling idea—speed and space. Each time, Juan encounters the foreign women in his traveling; for these female figures, Juan is also a stranger who makes them react in an emotional way and sometimes be counter to such an exotic lover at the same time. And we can see *Don Juan*'s journey theme has speed due to its shifting tone which creates the ceaseless points of view of sexuality and emotion. The space of the poem is continually expanded to make the journey an area where we see a kaleidoscopic way of Byron's intention on women-Juan relations and love.

Judging from the mobile tone of narration and digression in *Don Juan*, I believe that Byron combines his thinking with the form of the poem. In other words, the free style of its form underlies Byron's liberal concept toward human equality. However, Byron never entirely abandons a "romantic" mode for a "satirical" one. He just uses special rhetoric to convey his ideal love relationship between both genders. *Don Juan* is a romantic poem whereby individuals could grasp their natural feelings toward desires and love. And through Byron's depiction of love, we see the difference between traditional relation-thinking and modern sexuality. Byron anticipates a more liberal position for both sexes, thereby encouraging women to pursue their happiness and find out their own values in their conscious individualities.

In the first place, I choose Byron's *Don Juan* to distinguish his adaptation of the Don Juan legend from its original versions. Byron's female characters are totally different from the ones in previous stories. This is Byron's sense of his long-liberal thinking—to long for a more balanced relation for gender politics. To convey this humanist goal, Byron adopts satire to reveal the true feelings in this poem, refusing to cater to any hypocrisy in human beings' nature. And the narrative tone fits what he mentions in Adeline's canto: mobility. Put another way, both Byron's thinking and the contents of *Don Juan* are presented with a mobile tone. The narrative in the poem is told from the perspectives of three persons—Byron the poet, Don Juan, and the narrator. And the digressive setting is also used to be a foil for Byron's true concern of issues of love and both sexes. Thus, mobility, the representation of Byron's kaleidoscopic view, is a function of revealing his attitudes toward the old value systems and the supposedly revised condition nowadays. Then, the constant traveling furthermore strengthens the feeling of loss. As a foreigner, Juan's sexual encounter brings himself a new perception of love. And these women definitely show their sexualities in a brave way. Despite some of tyrannical aspects of these women, they are changed through their experiences of love. For instance, the narrator records Gulbeyaz's indignant reaction to Juan's refusal of her love—"So supernatural was her passion's rise, / For ne'er till now she knew a checked desire" (V. 134. 5-6). So Gulbeyaz almost wants to kill Juan for mitigating her rage. Nonetheless, Byron again conveys his true thinking behind the narration:

> I know Gulbeyza was extremely wrong;
>   I own it, I deplore it, I condemn it;
> But I detest all fiction even in song,
>   And so must tell the truth, howe'er you blame it.
> Her reason being weak, her passions strong, (VI. 8. 1-5)

Simply speaking, Gulbeyaz understands herself and would like to fulfill her desire in love. Byron's arrangement here is not to focus on her tyrannical aspect but her determination to pursue love. And her love toward the travestied Juan can be seen as a new possibility of homosexual erotics. Viewed from this, any love relationship is not subject to the fixed heterosexual love. Instead, the love relationship is unlimited and can be referred to any form of sexual practice.

After analyzing the female characters in the poem, I find out that all the women show their sexualities and emotions differently. Byron's usage of ironic tone to describe them enables us to see women's inner consciousness. Women may be naturally passionate, jealous, seductive and bluestocking-liking; however, they take action to seek a more unforgettable love. Furthermore, women build up their self-esteem and recognition more and more in their pursuit of happiness. Besides, the mysterious Fitz-Fulke and the powerful Catherine represent their strong desires toward Juan under the foil of gothic and war setting. Here women could really divorce themselves from cultural stereotypes about proper recognition of them. As to the pure Haidee, her love toward Juan can be seen as the most passionate one. In my opinion, Haidee-Juan's model tells us human beings should not hide their natural feelings but enjoy them instead. At the beautiful island, Haidee and Juan unfold their erotic freedom, which reveals the quality of love. Just like what Byron says as follows:

> The love of higher things and better days,
>   The unbounded hope and heavenly ignorance
> Of what is called the world and the world's ways,
>   The moments when we gather form a glance
> More joy than from all future pride or praise,
>   Which kindle manhood, but can ne'er entrance
> The heart in an existence of its own,
> Of which another's bosom is the zone. (XVI. 108. 1-8)

Here Byron again points out the importance of love and implicitly praises women's bravery behaviors to win their ideal love. Love which is not free cannot be seen as true love. Women's quest for their love results in elevating their confident individuality. Thus, Byron provides another more balanced structure between the two sexes. In so doing, Byron actually does not mean to satirize women but points out that women are not always seen as a second role in the gender code.

In order to describe the female dominance in their seduction of Juan, I use Kristeva's idea of "chora" to explain the struggled relation in their experiences of love. The women-Juan relationships are both attractive and repulsive, which fits the abjection in the "chora" space. Take Hiadee's love as an example, Haidee falls in love with Juan at first sight, but she uses different language to talk to Juan. And she also faces her father's violation and ends up dying in the island. Still, though Haidee's bravery shown in love ends with her death, love will be everlasting in her mind in that this unforgettable love is her own aesthetic experience:

> It was such pleasure to behold him, such
> Enlargement of existence to partake
> Nature with him, to thrill beneath his touch,
> To watch him slumbering and to see him wake. (II. 173. 1-4)

Byron's depiction of sexual passion and wonderful love just echoes Burke's aesthetic philosophy: sublime and beauty. According to Burke, the sublime is "productive of the strongest emotion which the mind is capable of feeling" (36), and the beauty is of "those qualities in bodies by which they cause love, or some passion similar to it" (83). These features are exactly the delineations of Juan and Haidee. In terms of Burke's concept of sublime and beauty, love makes two passionate souls unite into a boundlessness. The only difference in this loving paradise is that Juan is a receiver of love, and Haidee is an active pursuer. The power of love is so strong that it cannot be missed by the two young lovers. For Haidee, this is the extreme enjoy in her first erotic experience. Haidee's efforts to defend Juan are also a reflection of feminine dominant individuality.

While admiring the wonder of love, Byron describes a fantastic and awful situation that causes an extreme feeling of sublime and beauty. When a person falls in love, her beauty is shown not only from her face but also from her voice, body, eyes, and so on. Hence, Byron depicts these female figures in detail to show how they desire such beautiful experiences in love. In additon, Burke asserts that pain and fear "consist in an unnatural tension of the nerves" (119); these could be "qualified to cause terror" (119) and are also "a foundation capable of the sublime" (119). As a victim of love, Juan can feel such an uncomfortable feeling. In Juan's journey, the tyrannical Gulbeyaz, the despotic Catherine, and the weird Filtz Dutchess all make him feel unease. However, these female figures just broaden their new horizons and show their passions to their ideal lover. Through this point of view, both Juan and these female figures all experience a kind of unprecedented impact that love brings to them. For Juan, he becomes more sophisticated; for female characters, they become more individualized and independent in their seeking for love. In Burke's point of view, "[a] sublime experience is one evoked by something that confronts us with our vulnerability and is thus painful; however, the threat in this case remains at a distance. It is this distance that gives us the cognitive and emotional space necessary for sublimity" (qtd. in White 28). For both Juan and women, these suffering features in love are all kinds of horror in which they go through abjection and are given new individualities in the resulting process. Kristeva mentions that "[s]uffering as the place of the subject. Where it emerges, where it is differentiated from chaos. An incandescent, unbearable limit between inside and outside, ego and other" (Kristeva, "Suffering and Horror" 140). Hence we see that sweetness and pain are inseparable in love. Women accept this new stranger but struggle against him at the same time. From Burke's and Kristeva's points of view, love comes with pleasure and pain, but these special experiences give lovers new challenges and realizations toward each other. *Don Juan* indeed offers a revolutionary chance for women to notice their circumstances and cherish the opportunity of love. Even when they face patriarchal oppression or social stress, they gradually build their own aesthetic experiences in which their female sexualities are given a new power and their emotional desires are satisfied. Only when women bravely chase what they want can they obtain the freedom of love. They do not need to be subject to unhappy marriage or destitute of abstruse knowledge; instead, they have their own rights to enjoy their lives.

In short, women's sexualities and inner spirits of recognition are worthy of concerns. Through a male poet's point of view, we can sense a different angle toward relations between men and women. Therefore, we see not only women's dominant roles in *Don Juan* but also see more possibilities to represent their inner emotions. And the emphases of the poem with its own rhetorical nature have Byron's visionary implications. *Don Juan* suggests a way of looking at things from a good deal of "vision." Thus, the universe presented by *Don Juan* is of hopeful meanings and values. For instance, Byron depicts women's various types in their facing of love and probabilities to build their romantic, independent personalities through their interactions with Juan. In the opinion of Wilson, "[t]he world of *Don Juan* is a hybrid and complex creation of an author who yearns to believe in the ordered world that he thinks once was, but who finds an anxious, disorienting universe that he negotiates with questions, doubts, suffering and humanism" (50). I suggest that Byron's *Don Juan* really offers us a different angle to see the traditional orthodoxy of women. Life's possibilities will be richer if we reject the fixed systems. Likewise, women do not need to repress themselves too much but show their sincere feelings. Byron aims not to get rid of all the traditional values toward women and sexuality issue but just offers an alternative way of constructing a more balanced relation between both genders. The author's philosophical thinking toward freedom evokes a vision of revolutionary movement here—to show his concerns about women's positions from the previous periods to the present.

Through all the erotic atmosphere and female's quest for love in the poem, the gender politics are not fixed in the norm of masculinist domination and compulsory heterosexuality. In fact, women's identities are constituted in their social performances, and their powerful femininities are strengthened a lot. Likewise, love can be any unstable form in which people's interactions are based on the liberal standard. As the whole, I believe *Don Juan* presents a new world of balanced gender relations: it keeps the quality of the past but revises some concepts to reach a conception of freedom for human beings. With the depictions of love, it can be inferred that Byron really praises love a lot and encourages both sexes to grasp the chance to love. Put another way, people are born to love and not to hurt others painfully. Sometimes we will be hurt if we do not encounter an ideal lover, but we are not born to hurt others. We are born to love in this world. Thus, we should be free to seek the ideal love and then obtain bravery with the other lover. Women also need to reveal their emotions naturally, not seeing themselves only as a subordinate one in gender roles. *Don Juan* conveys such a natural feeling for human beings: to seek love, to feel it, and to set love free.

Judging from the form and the content of *Don Juan*, we can find out a free style of Byron's thinking. That is to say, his use of mobile tone and digression is represented in his creative work. As the story progresses, the narrator continually adds digressive topics to interrupt the main discussion: "But let me to my story: I must own, / If I have any fault, it is digression, / Leaving my people to proceed alone" (III. 96. 1-3). However, the poet's insistence on indeterminacy and arbitrariness of the poem is its style of freedom. In *Don Juan*, Byron's own love experiences are more or less the samples of the women-Juan relationships. Love is still an important thing in his life. As a male author, he uses the sarcastic tone to depict women and disclose the truth under the artificial manner of *Don Juan*. Through such a transformation from man's thinking to a woman's stance, he can think more deeply to realize women. Byron hates hypocrisy and devotes his whole life to liberty. With this liberal spirit, he reveals his attitude toward women and love: since love can be the whole center of a woman's life, she should respect her own feelings because love can direct many things, such as desire, thinking, action, and so on. If a woman always holds on the conventional discipline of being docile and passive, she will has less chance to choose the ideal happiness. Thus, we see Byron's depiction of female sexuality is very active, passionate, and even horrible. When he makes Juan a phallic woman in the harem, suggests the love relation in the mother-son relationship, or depicts other romantic situations, his aim is to convey the importance of love and women's subversion of sexual orthodoxy. I therefore conclude that only through such an emotional independence and active performances of female sexuality can women reach the freedom of quest for love. Also, love is a desire of beauty and a feeling of sublime. From these delineations of amorous atmosphere, we could understand a kind of life permeated with love is totally not a waste to a healthy human being.

Byron tries to tell readers that seizing the time to love is very important. Especially as a woman, she should bravely chase her happiness regardless of gender, class, race, and other oppressive elements because love is a strong feeling which happens in a sudden moment without reasons or explanations. At last, Byron's attitude toward love echoes the typical thinking of Romanticism—"Sentimental emotion is over everything"—the strength and extreme value of love can save both men and women. Therefore, true freedom and fulfillment for women do contribute to equality between men and women.

Works Cited

Abrams, Meyer H. *The Mirror and the Lamp: Romantic Theory and the Critical Tradition*. New York: W. W. Norton, 1958.

---, ed. *English Romantic Poets: Modern Essays in Criticism*. New York: Oxford UP, 1974.

Bakhtin, Mikhail. *Problems of Dostoevsky's Poetics*. Ed. and Trans. Caryl Emerson. Minneapolis: Minnesota UP, 1984.

Barton, Anne. *Byron: Don Juan*. Cambridge: Cambridge UP, 1992.

Beauvoir, Simone de. *The Second Sex*. Ed. and Trans. H. M. Parshley. New York: Vintage Books, 1989.

Beaty, Frederick L. "The Narrator as Satiric Device in *Don Juan*." *Byron the Satirist*. Ed. Frederick L. Beaty. Dekalb: Northern Illinois UP, 1926. 123-64.

Beatty, Bernard. "Aurora Raby." *Byron's Don Juan*. Ed. Bernard Beatty. London: Croom Helm, 1985. 137-219.

Bloom, Harold. Introduction. *George Gordon, Lord Byron*. Ed. and Intro. Harold Bloom. New York: Chelsea House, 1986. 1-38.

---. *The Visionary Company: A Reading of English Romantic Poetry*. Ithaca: Cornell UP, 1971.

---, ed. *Lord Byron*. Philadelphia: Chelsea House, 2004.

---, ed. *Lord Byron's Don Juan*. New York: Chelsea House, 1987.

---, ed. *Romanticism and Consciousness: Essays in Criticism*. New York: Norton, 1970.

Bostetter, Edward E., ed. *Don Juan: A Collection of Critical Essays*. Englewood Cliffs, N.J.: Prentice-Hall, 1969.

Botting, Fred. *Gothic*. London & New York: Routledge, 1996.

Boyd, Elizabeth French. *Byron's Don Juan: A Critical Study*. New York: Humanities, 1958.

Brecknock Albert. *Byron: A Study of the Poet in the Light of New Discoveries*. New York: Haskell, 1967.

Briscoe, Walter A. *Byron: The Poet*. New York: Haskell, 1967.

Burke, Edmund. *A Philosophical Enquiry into the Origin of Our Ideas of the Sublime and Beautiful*. Ed. Adam Phillips. New York: Oxford UP, 1990.

Butler, Judith. *Gender Trouble: Feminism and the Subversion of Identity*. New York: Routledge, 1990.

Butler, Marilyn. *The Romantics, Rebels & Reactionaries*. New York: Oxford UP, 1981.

Bygrave, Stephen. "Reading Byron." *Romantic Writings*. Ed. Stephen Bygrave. London: Routeledge, 1996. 161-81.

Byron, George Gordon. *Don Juan*. London: Penguin, 1973.

Cardwell, Richard A., ed. *Lord Byron the European: Essays from the International Byron Society*. New York: Edwin

Mellen, 1997.

Castle, Terry. "Eros and Liberty at the English Masquerade, 1710-90." *Eighteenth-Century Studies* 17 (1983-84): 156-76.

---. *Masquerade and Civilization: The Carnivalesque in Eighteenth-Century English Culture and Fiction*. London: Methuen, 1986.

Chase, Cynthia. "Introduction." *Romanticism*. Ed. and Intro. Cynthia Chase. London & New York: Longman, 1993. 1-42.

Chew, Samuel C. *Byron in England*. New York: Russell, 1965.

Christensen, Jerome. *Lord Byron's Strength: Romantic Writing and Commercial Society*. Baltimore & London: The Johns Hopkins UP, 1993.

Clubbe, John and Ernest J. Lovell, Jr. "Byron as A Romantic Poet." *English Romanticism: The Grounds of Belief*. London: Macmillan, 1983. 93-114.

Cooper, Stephen. "Beyond All Contradiction: Aurora Raby and Containment in Byron's *Don Juan*." *Keats-Shelley Journal* 38 (1989): 23-25.

Coote, Stephen. *Byron: The Making of A Myth*. London: The Bodley Head, 1988.

Creed, Barbara. "Kristeva, Femininity, Abjection." *The Horror Reader*. Ed. Ken Gelder. New York: Routledge, 2000. 64-70.

Curran, Stuart, ed. *The Cambridge Companion to British Romanticism*. New York: Cambridge UP, 1993.

Donelan, Charles. *Romanticism and Male Fantasy in Byron's Don Juan: A Marketable Vice*. New York: St. Martin, 2000.

England, A. B. *Byron's Don Juan and Eighteenth-Century Literature: A Study of Some Rhetorical Continuities and Discontinuities*. London: Associated UP, 1975.

Felski, Rita. *Beyond Feminist Aesthetics: Feminist Literature and Social Change*. Cambridge: Harvard UP, 1989.

Ferber, Michael. *A Dictionary of Literary Symbols*. London: Cambridge UP, 1999.

Foucault, Michel. *The History of Sexuality*. Volume 1. Trans. Robert Hurley. New York: Vintage, 1990.

---. *Discipline and Punish: The Birth of the Prison*. Trans. Alan Sheridan. New York: Pantheon Books, 1977.

Franklin, Caroline. "Juan's Sea Changes: Class, Race and Gender in Byron's *Don Juan*." *Don Juan*. Ed. Nigel Wood. Buckingham: Open UP, 1993. 56-89.

---. " 'Quiet Cruising o'er the Ocean Woman': Byron's *Don Juan* and the Woman Question." *Byron*. Ed. Jane Stabler. London: Longman, 1998. 79-93.

---. *Byron's Heroines*. New York: Oxford UP, 1992.

---. *Byron: A Literary Life*. New York: St. Martin, 2000.

Frye, Northrop. "The Romantic Myth." *A Study of English*

Romanticism. Chicago: U of Chicago P, 1982. 3-50.

Fuess, Claude Moore. "*Don Juan*." *Lord Byron as A Satirist in Verse*. New York: Haskell House, 1973. 163-87.

Furniss, Tom. *Edmund Burke's Aesthetic Ideology: Language, Gender, and Political Economy in Revolution*. New York: Cambridge UP, 1993.

Garber, Frederick. "Self and the Language of Satire." *Self, Text, and Romantic Irony: The Example of Byron*. Princeton, N.J.: Princeton UP, 1988. 269-90.

Gardner, Helen. "*Don Juan*." *English Romantic Poets*. Ed. M.H. Abrams. New York: Oxford UP, 1975. 303-12.

Giddens, Anthony. *The Transformation of Intimacy*. Cambridge: Polity Press, 1992.

Graham, Peter W. *Don Juan and Regency England*. Charlottesville and London: UP of Virginia, 1990.

Gross, Jonathan David. *Byron: The Erotic Liberal*. New York: Rowman & Littlefield, 2001.

Gross, Elizabeth. "The Body of Signification." *Abjection, Melancholia and Love: The Work of Julia Kristeva*. Eds. John Fletcher and Andrew Benjamin. London: Routledge, 1990. 80-103.

Grosz, Elizabeth. *Jacques Lacan: A Feminist Introduction*. New York: Routledge, 1990.

Hall, Jean. "Byron: The Surface Self." *A Mind That Feeds Upon*

Infinity: The Deep Self in English Romantic Poetry. London and Toronto: Associated UP, 1991. 110-31.

Haslett, Moyra. *Byron's Don Juan and the Don Juan Legend*. New York: Oxford UP, 1997.

Hoagwood, Terence Allan. "Culture, Convention, and Indeterminacy." *Byron's Dialectic: Skepticism and the Critique of Culture*. London: Associated UP, 1993. 34-99.

Hofkosh, Sonia. "The Writer's Ravishment: Byron's Body Politics." *Sexual Politics and the Romantic Author*. New York: Cambridge UP, 1998. 36-64.

Irigaray, Luce. "This Sex Which Is Not One." *A Reader in Feminist Knowledge*. Ed. Sneja Gunew. New York: Routledge, 1991. 204-11.

Jack, Ian Robert James. "Byron." *English Literature 1815-1832*. Oxford: Clarendon Press, 1963. 49-76.

Jackson, J. R. de J. "Reappraisals of Society." *Poetry of the Romantic Period*. London: Routledge & Kegan Paul, 1980. 154-86.

Jackson, Stevi. "The Social Construction of Female Sexuality." *Feminism and Sexuality: A Reader*. Eds. Stevi Jackson and Sue Scott. New York: Columbia UP, 1996. 62-73.

Jump, John, ed. *Childe Harold's Pilgrimage and Don Juan: A Casebook*. London: Macmillan, 1973.

Kaplan, Cora. *Sea Change: Essays on Culture and Feminism*.

New York: Open UP, 1990.

Kristeva, Julia. *Strangers to Ourselves*. Trans. Leon S. Roudiez. New York: Columbia UP, 1991.

---. "Approaching Abjection." *Powers of Horror: An Essay on Abjection*. Trans. Leon S. Roudiez. New York: Columbia UP, 1982. 1-31.

---. "Suffering and Horror." *Powers of Horror: An Essay on Abjection*. Trans. Leon S. Roudiez. New York: Columbia UP, 1982. 140-56.

---. *The Kristeva Reader*. Ed. Toril Moi. Oxford: Basil Blackwell, 1986.

---. "Women's Time." *The Feminist Reader: Essays in Gender and the Politics of Literary Criticism*. Eds. Catherine Belsey and Jane Moore. Cambridge: Blackwell, 1997. 197-217.

Kroeber, Karl. *Romantic Narrative Art*. London: U of Wisconsin P, 1966.

---. "Narrative Infolding, Unfolding." *British Romantic Art*. Berkeley: U of California P, 1986. 197-223.

Labbe, Jacqueline M. *Romantic Visualities: Landscape, Gender and Romanticism*. New York: Palgrave, 1998.

Lang, Cecil Y. "Narcissus Jilted: Byron, *Don Juan*, and the biographical Imperative." *Historical Studies and Literary Criticism*. Ed. Jerome J. McGann. London: U of Wisconsin

P, 1985. 143-79.

Lechte, John. "Horror, Love, Melancholy." *Julia Kristeva*. Ed. Christopher Norris. London: Routledge, 1990. 157-98.

Leitch, Vincent B, et al. *The Norton Anthology of Theory and Criticism*. New York: Norton, 2001.

Lorde, Audre. *Sister Outsider: Essays and Speeches*. Calif.: The Crossing Press, 2001.

Lovell, Earnest J., ed. *His Very Self and Voice: Collected Conversations of Lord Byron*. New York: Macmillan, 1954.

---. *Byron: The Record of A Quest*. Hamden: Archon Books, 1966.

Manning, Peter J. "The Byronic Hero as Little Boy." *Lord Byron's Don Juan*. Ed. Harold Bloom. New York: Chelsea House, 1987. 43-65.

---. "*Don Juan* and Byron's Imperceptiveness to the English Word." *Critical Essays on Lord Byron*. Ed. Robert F. Gleckner. Boston: G. K. Hall & Co., 1991. 109-33.

Marchand, Leslie A. *Byron: A Portrait*. Chicago: U of Chicago P, 1970.

---. *Byron's Poetry: A Critical Introduction*. Cambridge: Harvard UP, 1965.

Marshall, William H. "Beppo and the Structure of *Don Juan*." *The Stucture of Byron's Major Poems*. Philadelphia: U of Pennsylvania P, 1962. 167-77.

Martin, Philip W. "Reading *Don Juan* with Bakhtin." *Don Juan*. Ed. Nigel Wood. Buckingham: Open UP, 1993. 56-89.

Mcconnell, Frank D. *Byron's Poetry*. New York: Norton, 1978.

Mcgann, Jerome J. *Fiery Dust: Byron's Poetic Development*. Chicago: U of Chicago P, 1968.

---. *Don Juan in Context*. London: U of Chicago P, 1976.

---, ed. *Romantic Period Verse*. New York: Oxford UP, 1994.

Mellor, Anne K. *English Romantic Irony*. Cambridge: Harvard UP, 1980.

---. *Romanticism and Gender*. New York: Routledge, 1993.

Moi, Toril. *Sexual/Textual Politics: Feminist Literary Theory*. London & New York: Methuen, 1985.

Montag, Linda. "Byron's Allusions to Shakespeare in *Don Juan*." *The Byron Journal* 30 (2002): 29-37.

Oliver, Kelly. *Reading Kristeva: Unraveling the Double-Bind*. Bloomington & Indianapolis: Indiana UP, 1993.

Page, Norman, ed. *Byron: Interviews and Recollections*. London: Macmillan, 1985.

Paglia, Camille. "Speed and Space: Byron." *Sexual Personae: Art and Decadence from Nefertiti to Emily Dickinson*. New York: Yale UP, 1990. 347-64.

Phillipson, Mark. "Byron's Revisited Haunts." *Studies in Romanticism* 39.1 (2000): 303-22.

Price, Martin. "The Sublime Poem: Pictures and Powers." *Poets of Sensibility and the Sublime*. Ed. Harold Bloom. New York: Chelsea House, 1986. 31-47.

Quennell Peter, ed. *Byron: A Self-Portrait.* Volume 1. New York: Humanities, 1967.

Reeves, Charles Eric. "Continual Seduction: The Reading of *Don Juan*." *Studies in Romanticism* 17 (1978): 453-63.

Richardson, Alan. "Escape from the Seraglio: Cultural Transvestism in *Don Juan*." *Rereading Byron: Essays Selected from Hofstra University's Byron Bicentennial Conference*. Eds. Alice Levine and Robert N. Keane. New York: Garland, 1993. 175-85.

Ridenour, George M. *The Style of Don Juan*. New Haven: Yale UP, 1960.

Robinson, Lilian S. *Sex, Class and Culture*. New York: Methuen, 1986.

Rowley, Hazel and Elizabeth Grosz. "Psychoanalysis and Feminism." *Feminist Knowledge: Critique and Construct*. Ed. Sneja Gunew. New York: Routledge, 1990. 175-204.

Rutherford, Andrew. *Byron: A Critical Study*. Stanford, Calif.: Stanford UP, 1961.

---, ed. *Byron: The Critical Heritage*. London: Routledge & Kegan Paul, 1970.

Saglia, Diego. "The Spanish Canto of *Don Juan*: Writing the Carnival of Culture." *Byron and Spain: Itinerary in the*

Writing of Place. New York: Edwin Mellen, 1996. 121-49.

Shilstone, Frederick W., ed. *Approaches to Teaching Byron's Poetry*. New York: MLAA, 1991.

Soderholm, James. *Byron and Romanticism*. New York: Cambridge UP, 2002.

Stabler, Jane, ed. *Byron*. London: Longman, 1998.

---. "Introduction: Byron and the Poetics of Digression." *Byron, Poetics, and History*. New York: Cambridge UP, 2002. 1-17.

Storey, Mark. *Byron and the Eye of Appetite*. New York: St. Martin's Press, 1986.

Strand, Eric. "Byron's *Don Juan* as A Global Allegory." *Studies in Romanticism* 43.4 (2004): 503-36.

Taylor, Barbara. *Eve and the New Jerusalem*. New York: Pantheon, 1983.

Trueblood, Paul Graham. *The Flowering of Byron's Genius: Studies in Byron's Don Juan*. New York: Russell & Russell UP, 1962.

---. *Lord Byron*. New York: Twayne, 1969.

---, ed. *Byron's Political and Cultural Influence in Nineteenth-Century Europe: A Symposium*. London: Macmillan, 1981.

Tucker, Herbert F. "Recent Studies in the Nineteenth Century." *Studies in English Literature 1500-1900* 31 (1991): 793-842.

Tzu-yuan, Cheng. *Byron's View of Life Revealed in His Don Juan*. Taipei: Chinese Culture UP, 1986.

West, Paul, ed. *Byron: A Collection of Critical Essays*. Englewood Cliffs, N.J.: Prentice-Hall, 1963.

White, Stephen K. "The Sublime, the Beautiful, and the Political." E*dmund Burke: Modernity, Politics, and Aesthetics*. Thousand Oaks, Calif.: Sage, 1994. 22-39.

Wilson, Carol Shiner. "Stuffing the Verdant Goose: Culinary Esthetics in *Don Juan*." *Mosaic* 24/3-4 (1991): 33-51.

Acknowledgement

The three years of graduate studies in Hsinchu are the most unforgettable memories in my learning stages. With the greatest sincerity, I am thankful for my advisor, Prof. Steven Frattali. Thanks for his trust and encouragement, together with supporting my mind whenever I felt hesitant or depressed. I really cherished every opportunity to communicate with him. And his comments inspired my own independent thinking. Also, thanks to Prof. Andy Leung for his insightful suggestion and patience, which helped me be more certain about the Don Juan stereotype as well as the underlying meanings in each adaptation. What's more, special thanks to Prof. K.W. Yu, who provides me another angle for thinking of the Juan figure. Furthermore, I am grateful to my family. With their love and cares, I completed my book. I also know myself more and more. Thanks for the support from my friends: Alvin, Aaron, Charles, Amber, Christina, Kevin, David, and Jeffrey.

Through the three years of study, I have obtained many priceless sources and learned to be more decisive and independent in my thinking. Working experiences also enhanced my interaction with others. And participating in musical events enriched my life a lot. Whenever I finished practicing a musical performance, I felt relaxed and then excited to do my research more actively. I'll always keep these wonderful memories in my heart. In these months, I took some classes of modern poetry, participated in poetry club, and read a lot of literary theories. Regarding gender issues, there are many other aspects worth exploring nowadays. Indeed, Lord Byron really envisioned important issues of genders and love through his works.

Besides, the deepest thanks to the professional partners from Liwen Publishing Group. It's my pleasure to work with these kind people. Indeed, I really love myself and enjoy this book. Hopefully, you will also enjoy the reading!

陳正芬
Emily Cheng-Fen Chen
Taipei
November 2021